Restoring the Wounded Woman

Restoring the Wounded Woman

Recovering from Heartache and Discouragement

Melinda Fish

chosen books

A Division of Baker Book House
Grand Rapids, Michigan 49506

Unless otherwise specified, Scripture quotations are from the New American Standard Bible, copyright © The Lockman Foundation 1960, 1962, 1963, 1968, 1971, 1972, 1973, 1975, 1977.

Scripture quotations identified NKJV are from The New King James Version. Copyright © 1979, 1980, 1982 Thomas Nelson, Inc., Publishers.

Scripture quotations identified KJV are from the King James Version of the Bible.

Fish, Melinda.
    Restoring the wounded woman : recovering from heartache and
discouragement / Melinda Fish.
       p.   cm.
    Includes bibliographical references.
    ISBN 0-8007-9196-7
    1. Suffering—Religious aspects—Christianity. 2. Women—Religious
life. 3. Consolation. 4. spiritual life—Christianity. I. Title.
BV4909.F57 1993
248.8'43—dc20   92-44133

A Chosen book

Copyright © 1993 by Melinda Fish
Published by Chosen Books
a division of Baker Book House Company
P.O. Box 6287, Grand Rapids, MI 49516-6287

Second printing, July 1993

Printed in the United States of America

Restoring the Wounded Woman
is lovingly dedicated to
my mother

Merle Weir Wilson

If all women had a mother like her,
perhaps this book would not be necessary.

• • • • • • • • • •

Contents

Acknowledgments

My special thanks to the following people for their help in researching and preparing the manuscript and for encouraging me in the Lord:

My husband, Bill, and my children, Sarah and Bill, for their patience and help

The members of Church of the Risen Saviour, Trafford, Pa.

Mrs. Kathleen Roen

Mrs. Margaret Feaver

Dr. Sheila Johnson-Hunt

Mary and Elliott Tepper, David, Jonathan, and Peter

My mother, Merle Wilson

My mother-in-law and father-in-law, Gladys and Vinton Fish

Ms. Glenda Moser, Christian counselor

Jo Ann Marino

My special friends whose testimonies anonymously grace the pages of this manuscript

Jane Campbell, editor, Chosen Books

Ann McMath, associate editor, Chosen Books

Evelyn Steele

Linda Shore

Jennie Newbrough

Patsy Lennon

Sarah Phillips

. . . and the other women of Myrtle Grove Presbyterian
Church, Wilmington, N.C.

The Rev. Guy and Phyllis McCombs

My friends at Evangelistic Center Church, Kansas City,
Mo. , for their steadfast love and support

All the women who came to me with their problems who
unknowingly urged me by their acts of self-disclosure
to keep writing on their behalf

1

The Casualties of War

It was nearly dusk when our church's evangelism team pulled up in front of the modest white-frame home isolated on the Texas prairie. The card had read simply, "Please visit my son, Don. He's so discouraged." Perhaps, we thought, Don would be ready to hear about Jesus.

We were greeted at the door by a graying, middle-aged woman whose face bore the slightest hint of tired courage. She pointed us to the bedroom and retreated quietly to the kitchen.

We were not prepared for what we saw. In the bed in front of us was all that was left of her only son, Don Helms. The lower half of his body was completely missing.

As he had walked with his patrol through a heavily forested area of Vietnam, we learned, he and his buddies had come to a clearing. Wading through a rice paddy, Don had taken a step and heard the unmistakable click of a mine. It was the last sound he recalled before waking up more than a week later in a military hospital in Guam.

And it had been his last step. All that came home to his mother was less than half of her son. I didn't know, looking at him now, how he had survived. Everything a few inches below his navel was gone—his legs, his hips. Don would never stand or sit again. He would never marry or even leave his bed. In one cruel moment a blast had turned his body into a fragment and blown away his future. No prosthesis could restore, even in a makeshift way, what was missing. Don would probably lie there the rest of his life, isolated and alone, angry and depressed, visited only by his closest family.

We did not know what to say. A few of us made feeble attempts to reach out, but Don seemed too far away, too embittered to listen to the Gospel. Why had God let this happen? How could he go to church? How could he plan for or even look forward to tomorrow?

We visited for a while, then excused ourselves, driving back to church in silence.

I have thought about Don Helms often and prayed for him and his mother. Can God intervene? Will Don ever let Him?

Every soldier prepares mentally, physically and emotionally for war, while one or more in each platoon sees the joy of victory snatched by an enemy's cruel bullet. Don is one of thousands of wounded who came home from Vietnam alive but in pieces from a war that America spent two decades trying to bury in the deepest recesses of her conscience. People like Don have been buried there, too, buried and forgotten.

Emotional wounds can permanently maim a human being, too. Spiritual warfare leaves its own deep scars. Just as a battle wound can tear limbs from a body, emotional wounds can remove a person's zeal for life. I have personally taught, prayed with and counseled thousands of men and women over sixteen years of ministerial experience. And while Satan has focused in many ways on men, he likes to target the natural emotional vulnerability of a woman, subjecting her to victimizing forms of violation.

There are uncanny parallels between the ways women are victimized in the world and the ways they are victimized in the Church. I can tell you, in fact, that the heartaches Christian women face are just like those of their sisters in the world. The wounds Christian women face usually focus on the primary relationships in their lives and their own ability to bear natural and spiritual fruit.

Regardless of their attempts to reach their families for Christ, millions of Christian women leave the church sanctuary every Sunday to face in their homes not a peaceful retreat, but a battlefront of loneliness and heartache. They confront problems like alcoholic or drug-addicted husbands, husbands who do not love them, husbands who abuse them verbally, sexually and physically, husbands who ignore them by various forms of workaholism. Some of these husbands claim to be Christians and pillars in the Church.

There are women who live with the secret shame of addictions, women who became addicted to escape the pain of living. The single mother struggles financially and in every way to raise her children with little support from the world and sometimes without the compassion of a local church. The older widow has lost her closest friend to death while her children are grown and living in another state. The best Christian homes have wayward Esaus, prodigal sons who choose their own way despite years of patient upbringing. The victims of these heartaches are the Church's wounded warriors often left to suffer silently on the isolated battlefield of discouragement.

The wounded woman is a lot like Don Nelms. Unanswered prayers and disappointed hopes have left in her soul a hole where her faith used to be. An important piece of life is missing from her puzzle, a piece she thought God was supposed to supply. Her journey through life is now on automatic pilot.

Only going through the motions, she lives detached, emotionally and spiritually—shopping, shuttling children to meetings, cooking, talking briefly with her husband or others, watching TV, going off to bed. Christian friends seldom call her anymore because the formulas did not work for her. She is a painful reminder that life for Christians does not always go smoothly.

I have seen them in every meeting at which I have spoken, sometimes in large numbers, afraid to respond to one more altar call because they cannot stand to have their hopes revived and dashed one more time. There are multiplied thousands who have suffered unspeakable wounds at the hands of a cruel enemy with many faces, their spiritual fruit killed by an insidious blight. While other Christians "conquered kingdoms," these dear sisters were "sawn in two." While others' prayers seem to be answered, theirs are not. When they came to Christ, instead of marital restoration, they found divorce. Of the marriages that did survive, many of the husbands are still unsaved. Their children turned to drugs in spite of all their efforts. Their loved ones have not been healed as they were promised. Their problems did not fly away with a song or even the soaking prayers of the saints.

Many of these women do not even come to church anymore, or they come only out of habit, going through the motions of faithfulness, hollow and numb.

The spiritual warrior, like the soldier, is psyched for victory at every service. He or she is taught to deploy his weapons skillfully, to obey the Lord, to read his Bible, to pray and fast. But what if he or she falls in defeat? What if his prayers remain unanswered and his problems do not evaporate at the quotation of Scripture? Over him will step the fortunate victors who may have missed misery by inches and secretly believe they deployed their weapons more skillfully, or found greater favor with God.

For the wounded Christian woman, there is no victory cheer. She faces another ironic form of emotional pain, the added pressure of spiritual performance. While women outside the Church are not expected to have answers, the Christian woman must face her struggles with unflinching faith. And she must see miracles. When answers do not come, she experiences the secret sorrow of a disappointed heart often compounded by the well-meaning but misplaced words of Christian friends or her own self-deprecating thoughts: *I ought to have . . . If only . . . God answers others, why not me? It must be that I don't measure up.*

Maybe you or someone you love is such a wounded woman. Barren and afraid, you have been hoping that someone in the Church will see your pain and walk you, without condemnation, through it.

Restoring the Wounded Woman is for you. In it you will see the pain of other women whose struggles are like your own. Some are still struggling; others have found a road to peace and resolution with God and themselves.

In these pages we will explore the unique battles a woman faces, the weapons formed against her, the many masks her enemy wears, the special wounds she faces emotionally, the scars they leave—and, above all, the sure, quiet pathway to feeling whole, fulfilled and happy again. This book is no "quick-fix" out of trouble, but a less worn pathway to higher ground.

Take a moment now with the following quiz. It will help you determine your need for help. Answer these questions yes or no:

Am I Heartsick?

_____ 1. Do I feel pain over past hurts I am unable to resolve?
_____ 2. Do I often feel that God is withholding the answer to my prayer in order to punish me for sins of the past?

—— 3. Have I been torn from my mate through divorce, separation or widowhood, or have I been separated from significant others through unpleasant circumstances?

—— 4. Has my desire for prayer, Bible study, personal devotions or church attendance faded since I first came to Christ?

—— 5. Have I lost the joy of my Christian walk?

—— 6. Has it been a long time since my heart felt like singing?

—— 7. Has my perspective on life, situations and people become increasingly cynical, pessimistic or sarcastic?

—— 8. Do I secretly feel that if I do not try harder, my prayers will not get answered?

—— 9. Do I fantasize or daydream frequently?

—— 10. Do I spend a lot of time thinking about ways to escape my current living situation or job?

—— 11. Do I feel that I just don't care whether or not my prayers are answered?

—— 12. Am I angry with God?

—— 13. Do I feel emotionally numb over things that should affect me?

—— 14. Do I show any of the following signs of depression: A loss of appetite or compulsive eating? A sense that life is not worth living? Feeling less like communicating than I used to? Feeling more like crying than I used to? Irritability? Loss of energy? Self-pity? Sleep pattern disturbances? Difficulty maintaining interest in things I once enjoyed? Painful thoughts? Suicidal thoughts?

—— 15. Do I expect failure at what I attempt?

—— 16. Do I "close doors on myself," rejecting helpful suggestions, wise counsel, logical solutions to my problems, or do I engage in other forms of self-sabotage in order to "prove" I cannot do it or that God will not work for me?

If you answered yes to any of these questions, you show some degree of heartsickness. A yes answer to more than four of these means that you should seek help. If you are experiencing suicidal thoughts, you need professional help immediately.

Let's begin our journey together with a look at how you or someone you know has arrived in the dungeon of despair.

2

. . . .

Thrill Ride to Despair

Real hope does not disappoint the hoper, while false hope both disappoints and destroys. Telling the difference was Lynn's problem.

Lynn came to Jesus Christ more than twenty years ago, through attending a home prayer and Bible study group sponsored by a local church then experiencing revival. Couples were being added to the group as the Lord marched triumphantly through home after home harvesting not only the wives but the husbands into the church. As a new Christian and wanting to explore the limits of faith, Lynn began to pray fervently for the salvation of her husband, Jack. When several months passed without a sign of change, Lynn brought the matter before the Bible study group.

She was met with compassion as each couple prayed for Jack and assured her that God would answer. She would see Jack sitting beside her at church on Sunday morning very soon, she was told. Her hopes rose. She knew it was God's will to save her husband because of the statement of Paul and Silas to the Philippian jailer: "Believe in the Lord Jesus, and you shall be saved, you and your household" (Acts 16:31). Now, after the tender, heartfelt prayers of her friends, she knew Jack's conversion was not far away.

Lynn tried to help things along by leaving tracts and Christian books everywhere—even in the bathroom where he would be a captive audience. She tried to talk to Jack about Jesus, about how wonderful his life would be if he would accept Him. But Jack guided the conversation each time to a different topic. He seemed to respect her newfound beliefs but showed no inclination in that direction himself.

Becoming more desperate to see Jack safely in the Kingdom, Lynn decided to fast. But because she was pregnant at the time with their second child, a small group decided to fast on her behalf. With all this prayer and fasting, Lynn was certain Jack would soon be saved.

Weeks turned into months. Jack's name became a regular prayer request at every Christian group and service Lynn attended. With so many other husbands being saved, it was unlikely Jack would be passed over. Surely God was testing her faith. And if she could just believe fervently enough, Jack would find the Lord.

But her prayer group, it seemed, was becoming weary of her repeated requests. Sometimes they questioned her efforts. Was she being too overbearing? Was she being submissive enough? Perhaps God was doing some kind of work in Lynn. If she could just discover what it might be and change, surely Jack would respond.

Lynn listened patiently and embarked on a long period of soul-searching. What flaws lay in her character? What could she change that would please God more? Was she praying enough? Did she fast with pure motives? Was there something in her life she was unwilling to give up? What more could she do?

With every passing week Lynn became more confused. Other women had not had to go through this. The husbands of some had been saved the same night they themselves had been saved.

After six months of introspection Lynn was no closer to an answer. It was odd, because God seemed to be granting her other prayers. When she prayed for others, their circumstances often changed for the better. Two women who had been unable to conceive had come to her for prayer and were now bringing their babies to the nursery on Sunday mornings, while Lynn herself felt the sting of barrenness, as if her own womb were empty. The prayer she longed for most, that she was living and working for, remained unanswered.

Twenty-two years have gone by and Jack is still not born again. I met Lynn at a retreat this year. All the other women were sitting at our table happy and excited, while Lynn never smiled with her eyes, only with her mouth. When I asked her if I could pray with her about anything, she broke down and confessed a deep-seated anger at God and at her Christian friends. She had long since stopped asking anyone to pray for Jack, and they didn't bring up the subject either. She was angry at God for denying her the fulfillment of her desire for a Christian home.

At the same time, she and Jack had a good marriage. He loved her and was kind; he just never became interested in spiritual things. For over a decade and a half Lynn had awakened on Sunday mornings, dressed the five children and herded them off to church. It was she who read them Bible stories, tried to help them with spiritual answers to their problems. But of the three who were now grown, none seemed to have a desire for the Lord.

Lynn had felt bitterness harden her heart. No one knew the pain she felt on Sunday mornings when she saw other families at church worshiping God together.

Lynn was at the end emotionally. Inside she felt lifeless and lukewarm and wondered secretly if she had become one of the ones Jesus would spew out of His mouth. She could not muster faith and her hope was gone.

There are Lynns in every congregation. They attend every women's meeting and church service I have spoken to, ladies-in-waiting wanting desperately to see their most coveted desire come to pass, and ashamed because it has not happened. Sometimes they are judged mercilessly for a lack of faith. They are victims of spiritual warfare.

The Lynns of the Church need to know that other Christians understand.

Millions of women like Lynn have sought answers to prayer, only to watch their dreams shatter like a fragile vase into thousands of slivers that only Jesus Christ can repair. Unsaved husbands—some addicted to substances and processes that regularly claim their health, their lives and their family relationships—are only one of the many reasons Christian women despair. Another source of hopelessness is wayward children. Natural barrenness leads still other wounded women to conclude that God has passed them over in favor of others more qualified to mother.

Many women who thought their marriages would last a lifetime find themselves in divorce, even though they tried to follow traditional prescriptions for happiness. Many a wife has been rejected in favor of another woman. Financial difficulties plague women who are single, married and divorced, even though they tithe, give offerings and alms. Other women suffer in silence the wound of possessing a ministry unacknowledged regardless of the Holy Spirit's gifting simply because they were born women, not men.

All these women have come or will come to an emotional dead end.

Hope, the Vital Ingredient

In order for a woman to come to an emotional dead end, one vital part of her emotional makeup must be rendered inoperative: her hope.

Hope is defined in Scripture as the expectant anticipation that precedes true faith, since faith is the "assurance of things hoped for" (Hebrews 11:1). It is a vital element of real Christian love, for love "hopes all things" (1 Corinthians 13:7) and it is because we hope that we can endure. Hope revitalizes the soul and changes our countenance from sadness to joy. Hope is the reason the farmer sows seed. It is the reason people plan and work: because things will get better. Hope creates the vision without which people perish. And the presence of supernatural hope in the life of the believer causes the unbeliever to look for its source.

But "hope deferred [drawn out, delayed or prolonged] makes the heart sick" (Proverbs 13:12). It changes the emotional climate to despair, the antithesis of hope. By releasing her grasp on hope, a person is demoralized into passivity and taken completely out of the war. The lack of hope strips from a woman her reason to survive difficulty, to believe in a God who cares, to press on to see the reward of her faith and receive what God has promised her according to His timetable. Hope may even be the one spiritual quality that people cannot physically live without. Because hope is so precious a commodity and vital to the empowering of the human spirit, Satan seeks at all costs either to destroy it or to twist it into false hope.

The emotional experience of the woman with misplaced expectation is like riding on an amusement park roller coaster. Think about one of your childhood memories of a roller coaster or a new variation like the "Steel Phantom" at Pittsburgh's Kennywood Park. It is considered the number-one coaster ride in America by the American Coaster Enthusiasts because it

traverses, at a speed of 80 miles per hour, 3,000 feet of con-
torted steel up and down slopes of 165 feet and 225 feet and
through four loops, two corkscrews, two boomerangs and a pret-
zel-like helix that leave the prospective riders at the station
either trembling with anxiety or frantically lining up again. It
is the fastest, longest coaster ride with the steepest drop in the
world—one minute and fifty seconds of agony and ecstasy.

Satan, using various deceptions, helps the unwitting victim
onto an invisible roller coaster with companions unworthy of
her trust.

It is all-important, therefore, to discern the difference
between real and false hope. True hope finds fulfillment. False
hope leads to a thrill ride with an eventual end in despair and
passivity.

It was Lynn's inability to hope, after her dream of a Christ-
centered marriage had died, that led her to depression and
overwhelming anxiety. Here is how she was "taken for a ride."

The Hellish Helix

Lynn climbed onto an invisible roller coaster the day she
first realized the possibility of seeing her husband accept Christ.
It is only natural, after all, to hope that those closest to you
will come to Christ. With every period of prayer, Lynn's hopes
would soar like the *click-click-click* of a roller coaster heading
skyward. But when Jack failed to respond to her efforts, instead
of reaching heaven in the clouds she experienced a crisis of
faith, plunging at breakneck speed down the slope of disillusionment.

After each disillusionment came a brief period of sadness,
depression or grief lasting anywhere from a few hours to a few
days. Then expectation would start the slow, steady ascent to
"life as it should be," until another crisis, the realization that
her efforts had been in vain, and another race down the slope
of disappointment.

There were times Jack seemed mildly interested in the Lord. Once he attended a crusade with her, another time a men's meeting with a husband in her prayer group. Each time Lynn's hopes soared. But only days or weeks later they crashed again with unfulfilled expectations. Hope, crisis, disappointment, until one day her hope did not recover.

To women who are particularly vulnerable, the agony and ecstasy of the coaster ride may offer an addictive lure—especially for those who place their hopes in emotionally immature men. They find this kind of relationship romantically exciting and irresistible. Several Christian women have told me they were not attracted to men who were solid, stable and trustworthy. Instead, the element of the forbidden and dangerous piques their curiosity and kindles the spark.

But what a destructive fire is lit! They are seduced by a power stronger than themselves onto the ride of their lives, and left crushed and devastated. They may have trusted God to change their wayward boyfriend or mate, but their missionary efforts are like seed tossed to the wind. For them the roller coaster is one of trust and betrayal leading to the despair of breakup or divorce.

Lynn's emotions, like everyone's, were created to withstand the grief process only a few times in life. We were never meant to live in grief permanently. But a woman like Lynn who places her hope in an event beyond her control commits herself to grief as a lifestyle. When God did not work as she assumed He should, she felt like giving up.

Lynn, like a woman married to an addict, was doomed to end up in despair. Even though she is married to a husband who loves her, her desperate desire to see his salvation married her to certain emotional burnout. Women like Lynn, careening between hope, crisis and disappointment, are carried through mild or severe periods of mourning, which include all the stages of grief: shock, denial, anger, depression, despair.

Unlike healthy grief, however, the cycle is never followed by resolution. Instead, its victim is immediately set up to repeat the cycle all over again.

This condition is known as codependency. What does it do to a woman? When a woman like Lynn grows used to living in this emotional state, she is trained to expect hope and subsequent disappointment, followed by the grief cycle, as a normal lifestyle. Whenever she comes off the roller coaster through some form of detachment, she will need to find an entirely different way to cope with life. It will take a process of healing and restoration and a retraining of her emotional makeup to adjust to normal non-crisis-oriented living.

If she does not make that adjustment, she will spend the rest of her life emotionally numb or subconsciously looking for people and circumstances that will generate the old, familiar emotional responses she always experienced on the hope/disappointment coaster ride. She will become addicted to false hope or unhealthy relationships, or she may habitually seek out or create crisis. She will become like any addict who turns to another addictive substance or process, and God's real plan for her life will have to coexist with a labyrinth of emotional dysfunction.

The Dungeon of Despair

The hope/disappointment roller coaster is Satan's chief vehicle of seduction into despair. More dank and dark than the vermin-infested depths of a medieval castle, the dungeon of despair imprisons its victim in spiritual, emotional and physical inactivity.

After more than fifteen years of struggle, Lynn lapsed into a functional depression in which she lived passively for almost seven years. If depression, clinically speaking, is anger turned inward, then Lynn's anger at God and herself turned her into a spiritual catatonic. For days at a time Lynn would go through the motions of living but with no emotional involvement whatever. Appearing calm and in control to others who admired her courage in the face of adversity, Lynn was secretly bitter and hardened toward God and toward her Christian friends, especially those with Christian marriages. Her resentment slipped out from time to time through sarcastic remarks.

She had no desire to pray. Why pray? God could not be trusted to answer. Why read the Bible? It gave only pat answers that underscored her failure. Why go to church? Being married to an unbeliever was reducing her, she felt, to a second-class citizen. She could not serve God in the eyes of some even if she wanted to.

Like Don Helms, the wounded veteran in chapter 1, Lynn had become a casualty of spiritual warfare. Battle-weary, shell-shocked and feeling as though half of her were missing, Lynn had arrived at a place where she could not recover hope. Her emotional battlefield was strewn with the debris of unsuccessful spiritual warfare.

She had been immobilized. She had followed a step-by-step plan devised to separate her not only from hope, but from fellowship with her Lord. She had been targeted for despair, paralysis of spirit, soul and body.

Passivity: The End of the Line

Once the enemy has brought the Christian woman to a place of passivity, he has her where he wants her. Although he uses many ways of achieving the same end—from obsessive-compulsive forms of religious addiction to nuances of doctrinal deception—the most common way of bringing her to passivity is through the hope/disappointment roller coaster.

Jessie Penn-Lewis in her Christian classic, *War on the Saints*, describes passivity as the state in which apathy takes over the Christian, leaving him or her open to deception. Whether it issues from the waning of revival that causes a lull in the miracle-working activity of the Holy Spirit, or from a misunderstanding of God's time to bless and prosper, or from missing the voice of God and what He has truly promised an individual believer, the once-enthusiastic Christian begins to be enveloped by dullness of spirit and mind as well as (in some cases) physical lethargy.

Anger and disappointment over unrewarded effort, unfruitful witness or unanswered prayer dissipate spiritual fervency and cause the Christian to be swallowed up by inactivity. Since co-laboring with Christ is essential to the manifestation of enduring spiritual fruit, the Christian woman's fruitfulness can thus be thwarted. The roller coaster screeches to a halt, its mission accomplished. The believer is traumatized and stumbles from the platform.

Lynn's journey on the roller coaster of despair is multiplied across the face of humanity. But let us understand that bringing individual men and women, especially Christians, to despair is a tiny part of the conflict of good and evil, which will not culminate until the end of time as we know it. The wounding of women is one of the chief tactics of the devil to cut off the work of the Holy Spirit and hinder the cause of Christ in the earth.

In order to understand our personal struggles, then, we must place them in their true perspective. So often the pain we feel blinds us to the real struggle. Let us examine what a woman's purpose really is in order to understand better the nature of her wounds.

3

• •

The Barrenness Syndrome

Repeated cycles of hope and disappointment can bring a Christian woman (as we have seen in Lynn's case) to a state of mind common to many who love the Lord and have no conscious intention of running away from Him. It is a frame of mind I have come to call "the barrenness syndrome," because a woman in this state feels that her womb of spiritual fruitfulness is empty.

Fully realized, the barrenness syndrome is characterized by the presence of several elements: the inability to bear natural or spiritual fruit in some crucial area; the presence of shame, real or imagined; the feeling of being victimized by God in the common reverses of life; and a resultant anger and breach of fellowship with God. This breach may be constant or it may parallel the rises and falls of the hope/disappointment roller coaster. A feeling of victimization usually leads a woman to conclude that God's love is not constant and unconditional and that God has abandoned or is punishing her.

How does a Christian woman who loves the Lord fall into such a syndrome?

The truth is, many faithful lovers of God since Eden have found themselves in the very same emotional malaise. Such feelings may, in fact, be a sign of true intimacy with God. Hannah, Elizabeth, Jesus' disciples after the crucifixion, Sarah, even Abraham himself, the father of the faithful, all had their moments when such feelings overwhelmed them, sometimes causing them to take matters into their own hands.

Every relationship has expectations. And when these expectations go unmet, disillusionment sets in, and with it, anger at the one who seems responsible. The less intimate the relationship, the less likely we are to admit our anger. The more intimate the relationship, the more secure we feel and the more likely we are to express anger. Recognizing and expressing that anger—even anger we feel toward God—is essential to healing the breach. (More about anger with God in chapter 12.)

Let's look at how a pervasive feeling of unfruitfulness can result from one unanswered prayer.

The Source of Barrenness

Having recognized the work of the barrenness syndrome in my own life, and having observed its development in Christian after Christian, I have come to see it as a diabolical setup that first appeared in Eden, when Satan intruded on the relationship between the first couple and God. Man and woman were the crown of God's creation and both were given the same divine command: to cultivate the Garden in which they had been placed and to multiply, to bring forth fruit. The fruit-bearing part of God's assignment was the byproduct of their having been infused with God's own living breath and having fellowship with Him.

It is no coincidence that Jesus' prime directive to His disciples was to "go and bear fruit . . . that your fruit should remain" (John 15:16). Not only are believers to bear fruit, but the sign of that fruitfulness is that "whatever you ask of the Father in My name, He may give to you" (verse 16). The secret of fruitfulness, Jesus indicated, is the same as it was for Adam and Eve: "If you abide in Me . . . " (John 15:7). For this reason alone Satan moves into the thought life of every believer with deceptions and accusations that seek to sever that believer from fellowship with God.

The sense that God really does not have my best interests at heart is the underlying attitude of the barrenness syndrome. And anytime I come to feel that God is my enemy, Satan is at work, just as he was in Eden when he deceived the woman. God has been misrepresented at some time to every believer with thoughts like these: *He is playing a capricious game with my emotions. God doesn't really love me. He must be punishing me.* In such moments we often fail to ask, Why would God destroy His own creation, violate His own Word and victimize the creatures He loves so dearly?

Those doubts nagging at the borders of our consciousness are seldom thought through to their logical conclusions. Instead, we jump to the conclusion that God cannot be trusted. It is difficult to think about abstract truth when circumstances indicate otherwise, and the person who thinks it is easy has never been tested to the human limits of faith. But why do we jump so readily to the wrong conclusion?

The answer lies in the next step in the development of the barrenness syndrome: the appearance of a primary stressor.

The Primary Stressor

There are precipitating factors, psychologists tell us, that cause a person to become depressed. One of these factors is often the presence of a primary stressor, a major underlying cause of guilt or anger, real or imagined. The primary stressor gnaws at the conscience, subverts a person's good feelings about himself, God and others, and causes subsequent stresses to accumulate into a burden too heavy to bear.

We experience this daily on a smaller scale. We may have had a fight with our spouse, for example, and arrive at the office only to handle our work inefficiently all day, see more work piling up, feel (or hear) the reproach of the boss and return home to a house in disarray. The primary stressor is the fight with our spouse. The secondary stressors—the pile of work at the office, the sense of not pleasing the boss and the messy house—accumulate until we blow up or become depressed, turning our anger inward.

The presence of a primary stressor in a relationship hinders our ability to cope with smaller stresses. But what if the primary stressor is something more serious, something like marital unfaithfulness, a hidden addiction or an uncontrollable character flaw? In these cases the consequences are more serious.

The concept of a primary stressor also translates into the spiritual realm. Let's say that the primary stressor for a person is a distorted view of God and His love for him or her. Such a distorted view may come from the deepest primary guilt—an unregenerate heart that has never asked for forgiveness from sins and accepted Jesus Christ as Lord and Savior. Before any other stressors are considered, this one must be resolved, for it carries eternal consequences.

But what about the Christian who, though forgiven and cleansed by his heavenly Father, continues to experience shame as a primary stressor? The root may lie in unresolved emotional issues of the past, such as conditional love from significant other authority figures, or experiences of abuse by parents, teachers or others whose approval he sought. Or shame may come from the violation of his conscience by sins that, though confessed, have never given way to feelings of forgiveness. Or shame may proceed out of feelings of guilt over things he believes he should have done, as he subconsciously replays the "tapes" his parents programmed into him.

The most prevalent primary stressor in the lives of many Christians affected by the barrenness syndrome is the gnawing feeling that God's love is conditional and that He will one day abandon them. Even though God's love is assured repeatedly through Scriptures like "No one is able to snatch them out of the Father's hand" (John 10:29) and "I am with you always, even to the end of the age" (Matthew 28:20), the devil gets them to believe that God's approval is conditional on their ability to believe or to obey.

What if they have omitted something? Too bad, God's standard is perfection. Like a calculating CEO seated behind a wide desk, God is evaluating their performance, weighing them in the balances and finding them wanting. When the infractions become too numerous, they will be "dismissed."

But how does such a distorted view of God develop as the primary stressor in a Christian's life?

Legalism

Legalism was the religion of the Pharisees, based on a body of thought drawn from conclusions about the Law of Moses. While Paul, who had himself been a Pharisee, made clear that the purpose of the Law was to make us aware of sin and our human inability to keep it, the legalist tries to keep it anyway.

Every form of paganism is legalistic, based on the notion that God rewards good behavior and punishes bad behavior. Just as the Indians believed that thunder and lightning were signs of God's disapproval, many Christians react to God *emo-*

tionally the same way. When bad things happen or faith seems unrewarded, God must be mad or disapproving.

Before you protest, answer the following questions yes or no:

—— 1. If I fail to tithe or give to others, will I suffer financially?

—— 2. If I sin in word or deed, will I get sick?

—— 3. If I do not possess enough faith, will God be "unable" to reward me?

—— 4. Can I permanently "lose the anointing" by moral failure or sins of omission?

—— 5. Can I lose my salvation?

—— 6. If I fail to help others or if I sin against them, will God be "unable" to help me in times of trouble?

—— 7. If negative thoughts or words proceed from my mouth, will I bring evil consequences on my own head?

—— 8. If I am unable to conquer repetitive sins in my life, will God withdraw His blessing?

—— 9. When my prayers go unanswered, do I look for the reason?

—— 10. If I cannot find a way to stop my besetting sin, will demons be allowed to torment me?

If these questions made you uncomfortable, or if you answered yes to three or more of them, it is likely that you have been trapped, at least emotionally, into performance-based Christianity. It is also possible—though this may be hard for you to swallow—that how you feel about your relationship with God may be little different from how a pagan feels! Your attitudes about other Christians are probably judgmental and exacting. And you are being robbed and set up for the barrenness syndrome.

Naomi

The belief that God is angry with me, that He is playing a cruel game of "tit for tat," is very old and refuted many times in the Old Testament. Moses, Abraham, Naaman the Syrian and Job all learned that God's love is unconditional.

But one of the most inspiring stories in the Word of God is the story of God's intervention in the life of a poor widow named Naomi. Her story is found in the book of Ruth. If anyone was ever set up for the barrenness syndrome, it was this woman whose name means "pleasant." Her life had been anything but pleasant.

The scorching winds of famine had brought hunger and deprivation to Israel in the time when judges governed. Many Israelites had left the Promised Land in search of food, and it was this search that created Naomi's primary stressor. Her husband, Elimelech, chose Moab for their family's place of refuge.

The Moabites had fallen out of favor with God when they failed to help with food and water as the Israelites came out of Egypt. And the Moabites had been enemies of Israel since the time they had hired Balaam to curse Israel. "No . . . Moabite shall enter the assembly of the Lord," God had warned. "None of their descendants, even to the tenth generation, shall ever enter the assembly of the Lord. . . . You shall never seek their peace or their prosperity all your days" (Deuteronomy 23:3, 6).

This portion of Scripture probably haunted Naomi and served as the basis for her belief that she had fallen out of favor with God. Not only had she been victimized by a God-sent famine in Israel, but the place her husband had brought her and their two sons was a land toward which God's disapproval had been recorded clearly in Scripture. Naomi's primary stressor was firmly placed: Seeking refuge in a land God hated must have caused His favor to depart from her life. Little wonder, then, that after a time Elimelech died.

Times seemed better when Mahlon and Chilion, her sons, found love and happiness in Moab. They took Moabite women as wives, Orpah and Ruth, and were living happily ever after until the dream shattered. The two sons died premature deaths, compounding Naomi's sorrow to unbearable proportions. With these secondary stressors, Naomi finally concluded that a return to Bethlehem was the only course of action that might remove the curse from her miserable life.

Is this stretching the story? Hardly. Naomi's own words in the first chapter of Ruth reveal her conclusions about famine, life and death and her underlying conviction that struggle and deprivation would always be hers. Five times in this chapter Naomi's words reveal her belief that she was under the judgment of God: "The hand of the Lord has gone forth against me. . . . The Almighty has dealt very bitterly with me. . . . The Lord has brought me back empty. . . . The Lord has witnessed against me. . . . The Almighty has afflicted me."

Harder to understand is Naomi's distorted perception of her condition during the famine in Israel before she went to Moab: "I went out full. . . . " As though she had forgotten how empty their stomachs had been when the livelihood of Bethlehem, their small agrarian community, had been subtracted by drought and ensuing famine.

Present stressors indeed have the capacity to dull our memories of the painful past. The Israelites forgot the slavery of Egypt, longing for its "leeks, onions and garlic . . . "—much as the "sow returns to wallowing in the mire" when the believer's life proves boring or unfruitful. The knowledge of God's displeasure seems the only logical conclusion to draw.

But oh, how wrong Naomi proved to be! Waiting for a well-timed opportunity to show His mercy was her loving, faithful God. Her restoration came through the loyal friendship of one of her Moabite daughters-in-law, who believed in the grace of the God of Israel and eventually found herself participating not only in the assembly of the Lord but in the very lineage of the Messiah.

Legalists always forget the mercy of God. They even abhor it. Why would God act "out of character"? Isn't justice all God is interested in?

If that were true, Jesus Christ would never have come. Jesus Christ did away once and for all with the "tit for tat" punitive concept of God. His mission was to remove the primary stressor, guilt over sin, and restore humanity's fellowship with God by giving us His favor, which we do not deserve. This aggravated the compulsively rigid Pharisees. Their religious legalism shut out the believer from intimacy with a God who prizes mercy as His chief delight.

Legalism continues to separate men and women from an intimate relationship with God, because human beings still tend toward the pagan view that they are under God's frown. How did we develop this attitude?

The Origin of Low Self-Esteem

Human beings have suffered a low sense of self-esteem ever since the moment Adam ate of the fruit of the tree of the knowledge of good and evil. To the woman, Satan had misrepresented the knowledge of good and evil as wisdom, but in the awful moment her husband tasted the fruit, the eyes of both were opened, and they saw their own bodies and one another's bodies without the dimension of God's grace. Suddenly they felt ashamed and inferior. What Eve believed would turn out to be discernment—valuable in helping them fulfill their commission to keep the Garden of Eden—actually stripped them of their sense of self-worth.

Turning their scrutinizing, graceless gaze on each other for the first time, they did not like what they saw. They did not *like* themselves. And when they turned their thoughts on God with their new sense of "discernment," they didn't like Him, either. They became afraid of facing Him.

Ironically, they did not seem to react negatively to the serpent, as though the act that was supposed to enable them to tell the difference between good and evil actually destroyed their ability to discern true evil in Satan himself.

It is amazing how much damage is done to the Church in the name of this form of "discernment" that counterfeits the real discerning of spirits. The real gift, by the way, enables the believer to discern not only what is not from God, but also what is of precious value in ourselves and our brothers and sisters. When we can see only what is evil and rarely enjoy seeing what is godly, perhaps we have fallen for the counterfeit.

If you have ever been the object of such perfectionistic scrutiny, whether from a parent or teacher or another Christian, you know how painful it can be. No defense can help win back a viewer's grace-filled perspective of you. But further, unless you make a conscious effort to rid yourself of this graceless perspective, you will begin to see everything with a critical eye yourself. God and those He loves, including yourself, are judged mercilessly. Finding flaws and reasons for their misfortune becomes an irresistible pursuit. And in a feeble attempt to elevate our own low sense of self-esteem, we view ourselves with more mercy than we are willing to give our brother or sister.

Getting God's "Eyes" Back

Our sense of separation from God's unconditional love is tied directly to our judgmental attitudes toward others. If those attitudes undergo a transformation, however, the result is a cleansed conscience.

How does it happen? It begins by dispensing grace and love instead of judgment. By giving the other guy a break. By forgetting to assess the reason behind our brother's apparent loss, sickness or failure. By accepting him as he is and validating his pain with soothing words or silent support. By being like Ruth, and instead of reinforcing his expectation of abandonment, showing him faithfulness even if he does not deserve it. By representing God as lovable to others, rather than punitive and demanding. By loving others even when they seem to have acquired so easily the things we long for.

Where we have been reinforcing the breach between God and man, we need to repair it, making it easy for the prodigal to come home. Delight in showing mercy rather than taking secret pleasure in seeing others get what they deserve. Give your brother respect and honor, rather than condescension and patronization, even though this knocks the pedestal out from under you and puts you on an equal footing with him. He is going through the same trials and victories of life you are, with the same God on his side.

Everyone has his own area of private pain. I have never met a Christian who did not have some area of struggle over which he felt shame and a sense of barrenness. But how often we forget about our own area of unresolved pain as we assess cause and effect, sin and punishment in others! It is this tendency to judge that traps us in a debtor's prison until we pay the last cent.

Patsy, whose husband, Cleve, had to leave Bible school for financial reasons, finds it hard to greet Laura in church. This well-meaning woman chides Patsy continually for Cleve's leaving Bible school, convinced that the couple's current financial stress is directly attributable to this act of disobedience to God. But Laura, who points the finger, sits alone in the pew Sunday after Sunday. Her husband is an alcoholic who, in spite of all her efforts, has never accepted Christ or come to church.

Pointing the finger at Patsy is not going to help soothe her own pain. We may never know what an expression of mercy toward others would do in Laura's own life.

Sowing mercy in the lives of others gradually reattaches the severed cord of fellowship with God and changes our entire perspective of Him, so clouded now with deception and accusation.

It is not easy to change. Rigid doctrines have sometimes dictated a profile of God as "faithful to perform His Word," when what we really mean is that His Word is law with no mercy unless it is "deserved."

Showing mercy, on the other hand, opens our lives to an avalanche of mercy. When I stopped looking for sin in others, I started finding less sin in myself. When I set others free to be themselves, I felt God's acceptance of me as I am, without any need to perform. When I withdrew my accusing finger, I found out God wasn't accusing me. When I started loving and accepting the brother I could see, I felt the unconditional love of the God I cannot see.

But recovering from legalism as the primary stressor goes much deeper. Not only are those under the yoke of performance-based Christianity prone to judging others; they are prone to reducing the mystery of fruitfulness in a Christian's life to a simple, easily duplicated formula for success.

The Mystery of Peak 37

While sitting in a movie recently, the events played out on the screen poignantly illustrated this glaring deficiency in performance theology. The movie was *The Medicine Man*, starring Sean Connery as a profane scientist who, tired of the social politics of the university-based research community, sets up camp permanently with a primitive tribe in a rain forest in South America.

In the middle of this primeval existence, he stumbles onto a natural substance that actually cures cancer. But in spite of all his efforts to duplicate subsequent vials of the miracle-working formula, none removes tumors overnight except the original vial of medicine. When another researcher arrives on the scene with proper equipment, each vial is analyzed and its ingredients tracked on a screen, much like the peaks and valleys of an electrocardiogram. Each formula produces the same reading—except the original potent vial. At the bottom of its screen is a tiny peak, Peak 37. The rest of the film is the search for Peak 37—an unlikely ingredient that changes the formula from inert to powerful.

In the middle of the movie, I felt God saying to me, *I am Peak 37*.

It made me reflect: Is our formula for success simply the duplication of "surefire ingredients" that have worked for others, rather than the Lord Himself? Did the salvation of Lynn's husband depend on her doing the things other women had done? Does one church grow because it can duplicate the church growth formulas of another? Is one man healed because he discovered the secret of a sin-free life? Is one hopeful woman rewarded with a baby because she and her husband were more faithful to God than the couple who remains barren?

To answer yes is to trap yourself in bondage to legalism in one of its most insidious and subtle forms.

What does it mean, then, if your private pain goes unattended, if reverses come to you, if God's anointing seems to depart from your life, if blessings flee and nothing seems to come easily? Are you at fault? Is your performance deficient? Are your ingredients inferior? Should you be ashamed?

But the working of the Almighty in our lives will not be reduced to concoctions of our own making. This is witchcraft, the mixing of potions to produce miraculous results. God reserves the right to work on the basis of grace, according to His own timing and choosing, because He is Lord.

Removing the Primary Stressor

The first step in healing the barrenness syndrome is the destruction of the painful deception of legalism, which masquerades as sound theology. Once this primary stressor is removed, the presence of other stressors will stop leading me to the conclusion that unanswered prayer is due to some failure on my part.

Jesus, God's only Son, came to earth to remove the primary stressor, guilt for sin, from those who would believe on Him. Whereas a distorted view of God had developed through legalistic interpretations of the Law by the Pharisees and actually misrepresented God's character and intent, the cross destroyed that primary stressor. As we gradually renew our minds by the Holy Spirit as we fellowship with Him, abandoning legalism, the primary stressor of guilt for sin will be removed from our lives.

Will the fruit I long to see finally come in my area of private pain? The Christian who withdraws the finger of judgment from himself and others finds the secret of fruitfulness—resting in the grace that is in Christ Jesus. Abiding in Christ produces in every believer the kind of fruit He wants us to bear. Resting in Christ relieves the believer of having to decide what sort of fruit should come from his present situation, and it produces good fruit in sometimes trying circumstances. Rest allows you to stop striving for blessings of your own choosing and start being grateful for the blessings you have. The rest of grace lets me enjoy serving God because it heals my distorted view of Him.

It is a pleasure to serve God who smiles instead of frowns, who does not manipulate our emotions with threats of abandonment, who is benevolent and firm in His commitment to us, who always welcomes us when we want to talk, and has no intent, now or in the future, of judging or condemning us.

Can all this be true?

Jesus affirmed it when He said, "I did not come to judge the world, but to save the world" (John 12:47). Save it from what? From judgment. "He who hears My word, and believes Him who sent Me," Jesus said, "has eternal life, and does not come into judgment, but has passed out of death into life" (John 5:24). This is the rest of faith.

My Own Struggle

Several people have asked me how my two previously published books came about. How long did it take me to write them? "Fifteen years of pain!" is my standard reply.

You see, I have suffered the barrenness syndrome myself over the issue of church growth. My husband, Bill, and I came more than sixteen years ago to an inner city church in Pittsburgh struggling to survive. Its active membership was fewer than fifteen. For all these years we have experienced the laughter and heartaches of the hope/disappointment roller coaster as our membership has fluctuated up and down, up and down. After sixteen years of faithfulness we have about one hundred members.

Other churches like ours nearby are packing the pews, some of them asking me to teach their women's conferences and retreats, while the Lord's sheep have never flocked in such numbers to our church.

It is as hard for Bill and me to go to conferences surrounded by more "successful" pastors as it is for a childless woman to visit a friend who has just had a baby. I hate church growth books and seminars as much as other women hate books on *How to Win Your Husband to Christ*. And I understand what it is like to have people suggest areas for change in order to set our church up for God's blessing. It seems we have made every modification, tried every approach and tried to let God change our hearts, while our church is still topping out at about a hundred members.

Yet it was the painful lessons Bill and I learned from what some consider our "failures" that produced nationally published books on addiction, recovery and inner healing. Without this form of private pain and its accompanying sense of shame, this fruit would never have been borne, and the wounds of the people touched by these books would perhaps have been left open and bleeding. I am grateful that we have been able to see God at work in our despair and continue to count on the goodness of the Lord, no matter how hard it is day by day.

So it is with compassion and understanding that I exhort you. To suffer hardship and maintain your loyalty to God is of far greater value in His sight than seeing prayers answered to your satisfaction—something you have nothing to do with! Your faith did not produce the miracle; it was His grace that gave you His faith in the first place. Nor did your holiness earn the results; it is God's presence alone that makes a believer holy, again on the basis of grace.

Loyalty may be the fruit He wants you to bear in this particular circumstance. That loyalty (or whatever fruit we bear) comes in one way: maintaining fellowship with God who loves me unconditionally. And that means accepting God as He is, as Master of my life.

Maintaining fellowship with God would be much easier if the healing process were not interrupted by struggles with significant others. Does God, in the name of love and mercy, demand that I accept my role as victim and not discern abusiveness in people who may actually be damaging my relationship with Him?

Let's read on.

4

. . . .

The Warfare Begins:
The Violation of Woman

Take a pencil and answer yes or no to the following revealing questions about yourself and the significant man in your life:

—— 1. Did I/he grow up in a home where my/his mother was always honored and respected by my/his father or stepfather?

—— 2. Was he abandoned by his mother either emotionally or physically?

—— 3. Does he blame the other women in his life, such as his ex-wife, mother or significant other, for injustices or personal failures?

—— 4. Does he seem to need me too much, not giving me space?

—— 5. If I were to break the relationship, am I afraid of what he might do to himself or others?

—— 6. Does he expect too much of me too soon?

—— 7. Does he criticize me, trying to improve me according to his standards, either spoken or unspoken?

—— 8. Am I doing all the significant giving in the relationship?

—— 9. Does he need me financially or is he able to provide for himself?

——10. Is he jealous of my accomplishments?

——11. Does he belittle me in any way in public or private?

——12. Has he used any form of force, no matter how slight, to intimidate me?

——13. Does he like himself?

——14. Was he ever controlled or abused by another woman?

——15. Does he take responsibility for his own problems, faults or failures?

——16. Does he have trouble getting work or holding down a job?

——17. Is his demeanor toward me aggressive?

——18. Does he have rigid or firm views about women and their roles as being subservient to men?

——19. Does he attempt to use Scripture to attack me or validate his views that women should remain "in their place"?

——20. Does he believe a woman is entitled to equal pay for equal work?

——21. Is he possessive of me?

——22. When he is angry, does he swear at me, call me demeaning names or attempt to dominate me?

——23. Does he pout in order to manipulate me?

——24. Did his father abuse his mother?

——25. Does he believe it is manly to control or dominate women?

——26. Does he want to get "free milk without buying the cow"?

——27. Would I do anything to hold onto him?

———28. Is my relationship with him alternately thrilling and painful?

———29. Is he a true Christian? (Are you sure? The test: Does he show the fruit of the Holy Spirit in his life? See Galatians 5:22–23.)

———30. Does he support and encourage me to pursue the goals I have for my life, not only at home but personally, educationally, at work and at church?

———31. Does he respect, listen to and acknowledge my views as being as important, spiritual or valid as his own?

———32. Does he or would he assume responsibility as a husband and father or shirk that responsibility in order to pursue things more important to him?

———33. Do I feel used by him in any way?

———34. Do I have to change the way I am to be liked or respected by him?

———35. Does he expect me to return sex for what he invests in our relationship, even though we are not married?

———36. Am I afraid of him?

———37. Does he feel threatened by me or by my successes?

———38. Am I always the one who apologizes?

———39. Is he a heavy drinker or does he abuse other substances such as work, sex, gambling, _____?

If you answered no to questions 1, 13, 15, 20, 29, 30, 31, *shirk* to question 32 and yes to the others, your answers indicate you are developing a relationship with a man who is likely to destroy you either spiritually, emotionally or physically.

Destroying Hope

Can Satan enter a person you love in order to destroy you? He did in Eden, disguising himself as a serpent. Moving in unnoticed, he invaded the boundaries of Eden and selected the battlefield—the relationship between man and woman and

God. Satan tried the same tactic with Judas and even Peter in the hope of destroying Jesus.

Since Eden, Satan has never stopped slithering into lives, invading boundaries, setting up his own kingdom and taking what does not belong to him. We may think we discern his repulsive presence in others and be so very wrong, only to turn around and miss him in his most deceitful mask in the one closest to us.

For the Christian, Satan's target is our fellowship with God, our hope in eternal things, our ability to trust God to make something out of the circumstances of our life. Although Satan's tactics with men and women are similar, our focus in this book is his attack on women. Stealing a woman's hope breaks down the boundaries of her life that protect her family and her marriage, as well as her natural and spiritual fruit and her sense of self-worth.

In order to destroy her hope, Satan must destroy anything a woman hopes in. He will invade each primary relationship using deceptive and accusatory tactics. Since his goal is stealing the fruit from a woman's garden, and since gardens have boundaries to protect their fruit, Satan must wear down those boundaries or sneak in unnoticed to deliver his poison payload. The woman blinded to his presence in the man in her life is destined for heartache.

What happened with Wendy and Bud Milford shows how it can happen.

Wendy and Bud

Wendy Milford was an easy target. She had never been taught the principle of godly boundaries. The child of an alcoholic father and an "enabling" mother who submitted to his verbal and physical abuse, Wendy had only one role model as wife and mother—a woman whose life had been committed to emotional destruction. Wendy's mother, a Christian, had always believed that if she submitted to her husband's blows and verbal harangues, her faith and submission would be rewarded and he would come to Christ.

It did not happen. Not only did he not come to Christ, but Wendy's mother lived a tormented life and died at 51 of cancer when Wendy was 18.

She never knew that for eight years, from the time Wendy was ten, Wendy's father had violated her sexually. Wendy had learned to dread the coming of nightfall, for it was then that her own father would slip into her bedroom, into her bed and force her to perform perverted sexual acts. Her mother never knew and Wendy was too ashamed and afraid to reveal her horrible secret.

Wendy's mother was one of the 1.8 million women every year in the U.S. who, according to an article in the (December 12, 1988) issue of *Newsweek*, are victims of domestic violence. Wendy became a statistic, too—one of fully one-third of America's female population who are victims of sexual violence, and one of every five girls (as reported in the April 1991 issue of *Seventeen*) who is a victim of incest before age 18.

Wendy grew up feeling like two girls: one innocent and childlike, the other a filthy prostitute. She submerged the dark side of herself under a mask of angelic performance. Popular at school, always on the honor roll, Wendy planned to go to secretarial school—until she met Bud. Bud became her ticket out of a horrible childhood.

Wendy's walls had been invaded and demolished. She grew up having been cruelly violated in one of the most sacred of all relationships, the parent-child relationship. And she had learned from her mother the art of codependency: silent, needless suffering.

She fell for Bud in the last few months of high school because he was handsome and protective of her, and she expected her life to improve once the wedding vows were exchanged at the church altar.

But things did not improve. In many ways Bud was like her father—strong-willed and possessive. Unlike her father, Bud did not drink. He claimed to be a Christian. He was a handyman who worked sporadically and had trouble holding down a job. They had been married only a few weeks when Wendy saw Bud's temper unleashed in all its fury. He smashed his hand through the bathroom door, pulled her out of the shower and began to shove her around—because his dinner was ten minutes late.

After three years of marriage, Wendy was subjected to daily verbal abuse. He accused her of being a whore if she spoke to another man for any reason. In each harangue Bud swore at her, called her demeaning names and accused her of ruining their marriage.

But his behavior was confusing. Between his abusive outbursts, Bud could be very romantic. After his verbal and sometimes physical assaults, he would often apologize for his rage and try to make up to her with some form of penance. The new dress she had wanted or dinner at her favorite restaurant was offered as a peace offering, and the monster retreated behind a mask of the loving man Wendy wanted Bud to be. After a short time, however, he would turn once again, in this cycle of violence, into a jealous, vindictive monster.

The monster hated Wendy for her attempts to rise to her potential. Bud denied any possibility that she might go to secretarial school, calling her "a stupid dummy." He believed that women were meant to care for their husbands "like the Bible says." He himself had trouble getting work, even though he was an excellent carpenter. He refused to advertise, claiming that the Lord would send him work. Advertising, he said, was not trusting God.

In spite of all this, and after three sons, Wendy was determined to make her marriage work, to stay with Bud, to try to understand him, hoping God would change him. Several years went by with no change. Wendy did not believe she should leave him; it would be a bad example to the children.

Bud was also a church-hopper. They changed churches every three or four years. Whenever one minister became aware of Bud's abusive tactics toward his wife, he was blamed for attempting to break up the family, and Bud went on down the road looking for another minister who would validate his views on what home life should be like. Whenever Wendy, a gifted Bible teacher, felt prompted to share and was given the opportunity by the leaders of the church, she felt choked by Bud's lack of approval and rigid views. And as soon as she began to feel like part of a congregation, and she and the boys began to develop relationships there, Bud wanted to leave.

By the time the boys were in high school, they, too, treated their mother with disrespect. Believing their father's abusive words, they felt angry at their mother for turning their home into the hell it was—and angry at the same time for her taking his abuse.

Wendy was in her forties when the smile she wore to cover her emotional wounds finally faded and depression set in. Her only way to cope was to drop out of a life full of heartache and frustration. Apathy set in—toward God, toward the Church, toward anything spiritual.

Wendy had been repeatedly violated sexually, mentally and physically. Her marriage existed only on paper. Two of her three sons, now married, had opted to follow in their father's footsteps rather than follow her example of godly endurance; they treated their wives as their father had treated Wendy. Why hadn't God intervened? Why hadn't He honored her endurance? Where were the church and the pastor who could perform the miracle she needed?

Wendy now had no defenses against deception about God's character. She was vulnerable to temptation to sin, to find a man who would treat her with kindness. Her roller coaster ride with Bud had ended in despair. She wanted out. She even thought about taking her own life. Perhaps she could make it look like an accident—if she could do it at all. She had no money, no way to stand on her own, no support from her family—and no self-respect.

Why? Because Wendy had chosen a misogynist for one of the most significant roles in her life—her husband and the father of her children.

Misogyny

The misogynist is not a new breed invented by modern psychologists. The word comes from the Greek *miso*, which means "to hate," and *gyne*, which means "woman" or "wife." Various levels and forms of misogyny, the hatred of women, have always existed. The term used to be applied only to men who committed violent crimes against women, but it is being used presently to identify the roots of practically all manifestations of discrimination against women, violent or not.

Nor is misogyny rare. According to recent figures released by the Pennsylvania Coalition Against Domestic Violence,[1] one out of two women will become involved at some time in a battering relationship. The abusive acts committed will often result in physical injury and death. The same report indicated that one-fourth of all homicides in the United States are the result of domestic violence. In 85% of these cases, the police were called five or more times before the final assault, indicating an escalating severity in the abuse.

In every Christian gathering where I have ministered recently, several women in the prayer line have confessed to me that they are victims of physical abuse at the hands of their husbands. Many more are frequent victims of mental and verbal abuse.

Some women possess extreme feminist views and label all men who disagree with them misogynists. But the Church cannot afford to so polarize herself to the opposite extreme that we ignore the pattern and validate the misogynists in our midst, thus deceiving ourselves, silently supporting the abuse of women and quenching the Holy Spirit in them.

If misogyny is real, when did it begin?

The Warfare Against Woman

Misogyny began, once again, in the Garden of Eden. But the idea did not originate with man; it originated in hell. God promised Eve that because Satan had deceived her into committing sin, He would redeem the act and cause the seed of woman, the Messiah, to crush the serpent: "He shall bruise you on the head, and you shall bruise him on the heel" (Genesis 3:15).

But Satan did not slither submissively out of the Garden and into oblivion. He mounted all-out warfare, similar to his later attempt to crush the prophet Moses by the slaughter of the Hebrew babies, and his attempt to kill Jesus in His infancy by massacring the Hebrew children two years old and under in Judea.

Without omniscience Satan could not hope to isolate and surgically remove the hope of redemption from man. So he had to employ a cruder form of warfare, the shotgun technique. One of his chief battlefronts: the woman God created to help man. Recall the enmity God said would occur between Satan and woman: "I will put enmity between you and the woman, and between your seed and her seed" (Genesis 3:15). Satan set about to enlarge the hatred of women in the world in an attempt to quench out of her not only the Christ, but the

Helper, the Holy Spirit, who would come to reveal the Christ. Then help in its highest form would be rendered inoperative.

Millennia have come and gone. Jesus Christ, the Messiah, came, and after Him, the Helper, the Holy Spirit. Still, the demonic idea of misogyny flourishes. In Satan's economy, if a Christian woman is rendered passive and despairing through repeated hope and disappointment, good. If he can tear up her home, he will. If she is denied the right to use her God-given intellect and talents at home or in the workplace and receive fair compensation, so much the better. If she is denied an avenue for the gifts of the Holy Spirit in the church, chalk up points for discouragement. If she is deceived into destroying her own seed by aborting the next generation, this is in keeping with his diabolical purpose. And if she can be dominated by bad or satanically controlled people, especially a misogynistic husband, Jesus Christ is deposed as Lord of her life and she is rendered naturally and spiritually fruitless.

Wendy Milford's victimization by a misogynist occurred because of her own misunderstanding of God's purpose for her. Originally victimized by her own father and given a poor role model by her mother, she was particularly vulnerable to Bud's perverted ideas of what women and marriage were like, ideas formed by his own emotional wounds and Satan's well-planned invasion in his life.

The Invasion of Bud Milford

Bud, like Wendy, had been raised by an alcoholic father, a sulking, passive man, and a mother who spent her life nagging him to stop drinking. But Bud's codependent mother was more aggressive than Wendy's mother. Rather than suffer silently, Bud's mother screamed, swore and resorted to overtly manipulative tactics to try to get her husband to stop drinking. In the process Bud became a victim of his mother's verbal abuse. She would often accuse him of being "just like your father," a comment Bud detested.

Bud hated his father for being a wimp and a morally weak person, and he quickly developed the idea that his mother was the cause. Women, he believed, needed to be kept in their place so that these things would not happen.

Thus believing the notion that the significant woman in his childhood had indirectly caused his own pain, Bud grew up with a basic deception that gave rise to many twisted notions about male-female relationships. When he began his Christian walk, he superimposed his well-developed prejudices over the words of Scripture. Isolating Scripture verses out of context and picking up on the ideas of other men about women, Bud developed misogyny as part of his theology. Women, he believed, were at fault for sin in the world.

Bud believed that women were more able to be deceived and were, therefore, carriers of evil. They needed to be subdued, kept at home, prevented from getting out of hand and taking over. After all, didn't the Bible teach that women were inferior, that they should be silent in the church and that they were prone to usurping male authority? Bud's experience with his own mother corroborated this idea.

Bud had been invaded with deception by the time he was of marriageable age and possessed all the qualities that constitute the pattern of misogyny. His self-concept was diminished because his mother had abused him verbally. Partly by her constant nagging, she had expected more from Bud so that he would not turn out like his father. Under the weight of having to run from alcoholism and measure up to the standards of his mother, Bud had developed the tendency toward perfectionism in life and relationships and punished himself when he could not live up to it.

Self-punishment is the active ingredient in misogyny that actually leads to aggression.

The apostle Paul wrote, "He who loves his own wife loves himself; for no one ever hated his own flesh, but nourishes and cherishes it . . . " (Ephesians 5:28-29). The misogynist alternately loves himself with selfishness and pride and hates himself and others for not measuring up. Under the weight of this intense emotional conflict, the misogynist develops a violent anger that he unleashes on those who love him. He punishes them because they should not love him. His wife becomes his scapegoat by vicariously carrying away his own sins and failures that he lays on her with verbal, mental or physical abuse or with milder forms of disrespect. Thus, the contrapositive of Paul's teaching comes to pass: "Whoever hates himself, hates his wife."

The misogynist's pride releases him to play God. Like the mythical Pygmalion who sculpted a woman and saw his own creation come to life, the misogynist tries through using abuse to chisel away at his wife in the hope of developing her into his concept of perfection. He chisels away at everything from her appearance to her cooking to her housekeeping to her aspirations for herself. If he is a Christian man without a revelation of the liberty and grace of God, he uses Scripture as a chisel.

Women who were once beautiful have been transformed into shabby, dowdy shells because of their husbands' belief that Christian women should not wear makeup or fix themselves up. These husbands forget that Queen Esther saved her people by faith in God and the use of cosmetics! And they twist the biblical concept of modesty to mean that a woman should not feel good about herself or look attractive in public or in the mirror. He makes every effort to keep her under wraps.

At the other extreme is a misogynit's perfectionistic concept of beauty. The rise in plastic surgery is attributable in part to husbands' dissatisfaction with their wives' bodies. Her tummy is too flabby, her breasts too small, her nose too large. In order to gratify his concept of what a woman should look like, he pressures his wife (chipping away at her self-esteem) to submit to the surgeon's knife.

Several women have confided to me that it was their Christian husbands who suggested plastic surgery for them. It may be painful, expensive, even risky. The misogynist does not care. Uppermost in his thinking is creating a woman in his own image.

Possessiveness is another way the misogynist exerts control. In his world view, a woman cannot be trusted to develop relationships. One of the principal characteristics of misogyny is the isolation of its victim. Like an animal isolating its prey before the kill, the misogynist will attempt to cut his wife off from her family, her friends, everything and everyone important to her. If anyone invades his territory and tries to communicate with her, he or she is perceived and treated as an invader. Often the misogynist blames his wife. Bud Milford attempted to isolate Wendy whenever he felt threatened by other relationships in her life, particularly any leadership role, however small, in the churches they attended. Thus, Bud's repeated desire to uproot the family and church-hop.

The conclusion of the apostle Paul about women is that in the Church, women are elevated to equality by being clothed with the same Spirit who clothes Christian men. "For all of you who were baptized into Christ have clothed yourselves with Christ. There is neither Jew nor Greek, there is neither slave nor free man, there is neither male nor female; for you are all one in Christ Jesus" (Galatians 3:27-28). The gifts, callings and offices in the Church are not male or female, but manifestations of the Holy Spirit who is neither. Sexual differences pertain to natural man for natural reasons, not for spiritual distinction.

But Bud believed that Christian women were to hold their heads in shame for the sin of Eve and keep their mouths shut.

His demands quenched the Holy Spirit in Wendy, although she was an excellent Bible teacher and well-respected in every church they attended. Their churches missed out because of her husband's misogyny and Wendy's lack of understanding as to how to rise above it.

But Bud missed out, too. No one ever quenches the Holy Spirit in himself or others without missing important blessings. As Bud exercised rigidity and restriction, he felt the chain tighten around his own neck. As he quenched God's Spirit in his wife, he did not advance spiritually and reaped dryness in his own life. He felt he could not pray, that God was not listening to him.

In fact, the prayers of husbands who mistreat their wives *are* hindered. Bud did not recall the admonition to "live with your wives in an understanding way, as with a weaker vessel, since she is a woman; and grant her honor as a fellow heir of the grace of life, *so that your prayers may not be hindered*" (1 Peter 3:7, italics mine). Bud felt guilty before God because he *was* guilty. But he always assumed Wendy was somehow to blame for his lack of spirituality, in the same way he blamed women for everything.

Misogynists like Bud exist in the workplace, church and in virtually every arena of life, particularly where they go unchallenged. They have been led unknowingly into deception by their own emotional wounds and are locked in prisons of their own making. They live under the pressure of having to control every one of these arenas of life, oblivious to the help God has sent them in womankind.

But they would have no power if women like Wendy were not vulnerable to them, if women would learn what God's intention is for marriage, and if Christian women would learn the principles we will discuss in the following chapter.

5

· ·

The Christian Marriage: Its Rights and Boundaries

When God created man and woman, He wanted their marriage to enhance their relationship with Him. He wanted to see His Garden protected and fruit produced. But above all He wanted to enjoy their fellowship. "It is not good for the man to be alone," God observed. "I will make him a helper suitable for him" (Genesis 2:18).

God has not changed His mind. The highest ideal for marriage is a relationship that enhances each partner's knowledge of God, releases the power of the Holy Spirit in them and bears fruit that helps reattach others to God. This is why the apostle Paul cautioned Christians not to become "unequally yoked together with unbelievers" (2 Corinthians 6:14, KJV). To do so would subject the Christian to a fallen person's unenlightened attitudes and perhaps even make the Christian vulnerable to victimization.

When a person becomes a Christian after marriage, the Bible encourages him or her not to leave the unbelieving spouse, but to give God a chance to work in the heart of that spouse in the hope that he or she might also come to know Jesus Christ. Certainly this has happened many times.

If a Christian woman is married to a misogynist, however, the opposite happens. Subjecting herself to the satanically controlled spouse, the woman opens herself to repeated forms of abuse. As her husband's heart hardens in unbelief, the wounded Christian woman gradually loses faith in God and becomes fruitless and angry.

The same sad result can happen to a woman married to a man who claims to be a Christian but treats her as an unbeliever would treat his wife. Lost between the cracks in many of our Christian teachings about marriage are people like Wendy Milford, whom we met in the last chapter. While the Scriptures give clear instructions to women married to believers and unbelievers, what do they say to a woman whose husband talks like a Christian but acts like a non-Christian? Is she entitled to peace? How will she know whether to remain with him or leave?

The key to rest and restoration in her life is the establishment of boundaries around the place God has given her. It is an all-too-little-taught biblical principle, but if more Christians would learn it, Satan's ability to control their lives would be greatly hindered.

The Reason for Boundaries

Boundaries define limits. They place a secure border around what is ours. Everything outside may be in turmoil, but within our own borders we may conduct life as we believe it should be conducted and find peace.

God established the boundaries of Eden with four rivers. Within those borders, the man and woman were responsible for cultivating and keeping the grounds, with the further directive to "multiply, and fill the earth, and subdue it; and rule over . . . every living thing" (Genesis 1:28). Before the Fall Adam and Eve possessed what we might consider supernatural strength, the source of which was their relationship with God. Once that relationship was broken, their strength was gone. God drove them out of the Garden and established smaller boundaries and a lesser mission. Rather than govern the earth, Adam was now responsible only for earning his way, wherever he settled, by the sweat of his brow.

When Abraham, the friend of God, walked the earth, God gave him larger borders: the promise of a land. It was his relationship with God that determined his ability to walk about it and possess it. Not too great or too small, it fit his strength. He knew his limits because he knew his borders.

Every life has borders set by God. These are determined not necessarily by natural ability or even by spiritual prowess, but by God's grace and purpose. We all have a "garden" to tend, and by God's grace we can cultivate and keep it. Within our garden we have authority delegated from God to operate within biblical, godly limits. And we have rights that accompany that authority. The borders provide definition to our purpose in life, giving us all we can handle with God's grace. Whether it is a household, children, a career, a ministry or a mission field, each Christian fits into God's plan.

All warfare, natural and spiritual, is conducted over borders. In the spiritual realm, Satan attempts to subvert man's effectiveness by initiating confusion over his rightful borders. Sinful humankind always errs in his estimate of how much belongs to him. The person who thinks of himself "more highly . . . than he ought to think" (Romans 12:3) assumes larger boundaries and spends his life frustrated at being unable to care sufficiently for what he stakes out. Sometimes a Christian fares no better because he thinks *less* of himself than God does, thus shrinking his boundaries and never finding out what good things God has in store for him.

But the one who sees herself and her calling in God's light finds peace within the borders God sets for her. She is able to cultivate and keep that ground with the strength and gifting she obtains from her relationship with God.

These spiritual boundaries do not apply only to external things like homes and mission fields, but are predominantly internal and represent a guard for the spirit and soul. They are our moral standards, our consciences, and these boundaries must be established by God if our relationship with Him is to move forward.

Internal boundaries determine what we will permit ourselves to believe and what we will allow others to do to us. When they are not defined by God, they take us out of the realm of His peace. The unbeliever lives life aimlessly and arbitrarily with inconsistent boundaries. Likewise, the Christian whose internal boundaries are not set by God lives life with a guilty, compromising attitude, the product of blurred boundaries.

The person with no control over his own spirit is "like a city that is broken into and without walls" (Proverbs 25:28). His boundaries are constantly being overrun by forces beyond himself. He is vulnerable to invasion by Satan-controlled people and deceptive ideas. He becomes emotionally and spiritually devastated.

Without commenting on the political and prophetic implications of the Middle East crisis, let me simply point out the Palestinian people as a natural example of what it is like to live without national boundaries. Angry, belligerent, feeling violated, purposeless and vulnerable, the Palestinian people are broken in spirit. They have few rights and are regarded as intruders, unwelcome guests.

It is just this way for the wounded woman who has no boundaries. She has been overrun and left without a place of peace and security. And when she cannot take it anymore, she resorts to her own ways of fighting back, ways that are not always godly.

When Satan left Eden, he targeted woman (as we saw in the last chapter) as a main focus of his plan. The victory God pronounced—"He [the coming Messiah] shall bruise you on the head, and you shall bruise him on the heel" (Genesis 3:15)—came for the woman at a high price, perpetual enmity between her and the serpent until one or the other combatant is annihilated. Invading her boundaries has become, therefore, primary to Satan's success. He attacks her body, soul and spirit with his own brand of guerrilla warfare.

The Invasion of Wendy Milford

I want to return to the case of Wendy Milford throughout much of the rest of this chapter because her story has a positive ending, one that will encourage everyone who has been experiencing pain or futility from a lack of boundaries.

Satan had invaded Wendy's external and internal boundaries early in her life (as we have already seen) through her father's alcoholic rages and his incest. Once the primary violation occurred, it was easier for subsequent significant others, like her husband, to invade her life.

But Satan was also able to invade the boundaries of her conscience through her mother's false understanding of submission. Watching her mother be tormented by her father taught Wendy that godly submission has no boundaries, that a Christian woman has no rights in her marriage, that she is obligated to take whatever comes her way as "the will of God." These lessons laid the groundwork for doctrinal deception and validated the formation of codependency.

The codependent usually has no idea she is actually trying to replace the atoning work of Christ with her own efforts. Making sacrifice after sacrifice, giving up boundary after boundary to immoral or Satan-inspired people, she fancies that her efforts are bringing her abuser closer to redemption in some form. She may even derive a sense of godliness and spiritual pleasure from "laying down her life." But the one who will not receive the atoning work of Christ never appreciates the martyrdom of a woman possessed with a messianic complex.

This truth is illustrated in the parable Jesus told of the rich man and the beggar, Lazarus, both of whom had died. The rich man begged Abraham to send Lazarus to dip his finger into water and cool his tongue. When Abraham said no, the rich man begged for Lazarus to be sent to his brothers to warn them of the torment of hell. But Abraham replied, "If they do not listen to Moses and the Prophets, neither will they be persuaded if someone rises from the dead" (Luke 16:31). Jesus was saying that there are those who simply will not receive the good news of the Gospel, people who have already hardened themselves to God's efforts to save them.

About a woman with a messianic complex, then: A real martyr never seeks martyrdom, but only to obey Jesus Christ, while a martyrdom-seeker thinks her sufferings are adding somehow to what Jesus has done on the cross. But think about it: If a sinner has not responded to the story of Jesus' suffering and death on his behalf, is it not a strange form of pride for a woman to believe that making herself his victim will finally get the Gospel through to him?

Wendy, hoping to bring Bud to redemption through her own submission, and unaware of the importance of God-given boundaries, grew up believing that she, like her mother, was doing right in God's sight by permitting herself to be abused. Isn't a Christian supposed to go the extra mile? Turn the other cheek? Give up not only one's cloak but one's shirt? And isn't divorce always wrong for a Christian? Wendy considered her home her mission field, and that she was bound to lay down her life, if necessary, for the cause of Christ.

She did not realize until years later that all her mother's torment did not result in her father's salvation, that it only wore her down physically and emotionally, and that she lived a life blinded to natural and spiritual reality. Nor did Wendy realize—until her sons grew up—the alarming truth that sons who watch their fathers (Christian or not) abuse their mothers almost always grow up to be abusers, too.

Wendy's introduction to life had given Satan a vantage point. From it he worked to keep her in the psychological process known as denial, a pattern of thinking that allows women to remain blind to certain realities—including their own victimization.

Dr. James Dobson in *Love Must Be Tough* explains that out of fear of facing the truth, the abused spouse "chooses not to notice . . . in the hope that it will blow over and be forgotten. . . . When evidence becomes overwhelming, the victim will ask the guilty spouse to assist in the denial by setting up questions that seem direct, but the victim is satisfied with lies. . . . Through this process [denial] the mind is protected for a time, but it often permits even greater disasters to gain a foothold in our lives."

In trying to protect herself from the truth that her marriage is failing and that her victimization is in vain, the wounded woman allows herself to be invaded by the deception that all is well and will continue to be well.

Sometimes, unfortunately, Scripture is used to reinforce denial. Many Christian women, through a wrong understanding of God's purpose for women and His provisions to protect them, are vulnerable to deception and abuse. Wrong understandings of biblical submission are just one example. (We will discuss submission later in this chapter and in the next.)

Women distort the Word of God to their own destruction—the very Word meant to bring them life!

A wife's relationship with her husband can be elevated, through devious means, to a place of lordship meant only for Jesus Christ. She experiences the cruel domination of a sin-sick man as prophesied in Genesis 3:16: "Your desire shall be for your husband, and he shall rule over you." Because she believes that the Bible actually teaches wives to submit to abuse, she may harbor a deep-seated anger at God. And ultimately she is left empty and passive.

I know of one woman who concealed the abuse she received from her husband for years and taught the women in her Bible study this concept: "If my husband will come to Christ by the soles of his feet, then I will be his doormat." Over the years she was forced to live in poverty, beaten and abused. Then her husband left her for another woman. He did not come to Christ "by the soles of his feet." (No one comes to Christ that way.) Her husband will come only through his heart, which is now hardened to the touch of God.

The abuse of a wife is never the will of God. It is, rather, the manifestation of her husband's self-contempt. By acquiescing silently, Wendy was cooperating with Satan's attack, letting him invade her life at will.

Such invasion is handled properly by knowing your boundaries and enforcing them—not by natural warfare but by refusing to allow yourself to be victimized. The Christian woman must know that God is with her in drawing those boundaries in Christian marriage, and it will help her to know scriptural models for enforcing those boundaries.

What Makes a Marriage in God's Sight?

The first thing to understand is what marriage is and what it is not. Marriage is more than a piece of paper, a license signed on the wedding day. In few cases does the letter kill and the spirit give life so much as in marriage! It is by definition a two-sided commitment in which a man and woman promise to remain faithful and to serve the other's highest good.

Marriage is defined by vows that promise each participant rights. These rights naturally define the expectations each party has of the other. Marriage as instituted by God and nurtured by the Church sees man and woman submitting to God *together.*

The Bible states that the husband is the head of the wife (Ephesians 5:23), but this is often misunderstood. The word *head* in Greek is *kephale,* which means "source." The husband is to love his wife as Christ loves the Church, and his love will release his wife naturally and spiritually to liberty in Christ. The wife loved with this kind of love is to respond as the Church does to Christ, honoring, praising and obeying her husband.

A true Christian marriage is the condition of that union before God, society and the Church. A number of elements make a marriage a true picture of Christ and His relationship to His Bride, the Church.

Fidelity

Fidelity in marriage illustrates the commitment of Jesus Christ to those who have given themselves to Him. It is permanent, incorruptible, irreversible and reflected in the words "I will never desert you, nor will I ever forsake you" (Hebrews 13:5). Marriage thrives on trust that the spouse has forsaken all other partners, physically and emotionally, and that the relationship is secure until death.

But how many spouses commit adultery, hoping their secret will never be found out? If statistics reported by Oprah Winfrey recently are accurate, nearly seventy percent! And how many spouses who never go through with physical adultery commit emotional adultery by leaning on the marriage partner of another or flirting with someone else? God knows and so, somehow, does the other partner. Trust erodes and with it the marriage.

Sex

Marriage is set apart as different from all other relationships by the sexual bond. The Scriptures teach that each spouse has authority over the other's body.

The purpose of sex is more than procreation and gratification; it glorifies God and enhances love and closeness. Sex means little to a woman if she is not first made to feel loved. And actions even on the marriage bed that defile the consciences of husband and wife and do not glorify God have no place in marriage. Boundaries of purity and wholesomeness should surround the bed of a marriage if it is to reflect Christ and the Church.

Love

In Ephesians 5:25 and 33, a husband is commanded to love his wife as Christ loves the Church and as the husband loves himself. Such sacrificial, selfless love—giving as Jesus gave Himself for the Church—lifts the wife to a place of respect. This love is no kin to domination and control, which are satanic qualities. Such love is, rather, mutual respect.

Each woman's emotional and physical needs are unique. One well-meaning husband who was having trouble in his marriage always ran through a list of everything he was doing to make his wife happy. He was incredulous that nothing worked. But his love in her eyes was perfunctory. His chief mistake, as he desperately pushed every button, was not finding out from her what really pleased her, what would make her happy.

Provision

A man fulfilling his responsibility as head will be a provider. A woman committed to meeting her husband's needs has a right, according to the Bible, to expect that her material needs be adequately supplied. The man who "does not provide for his own," according to 1 Timothy 5:8, "and especially for those of his household . . . has denied the faith, and is worse than an unbeliever."

Nor is this kind of Christlike provision a mentality that condemns a family to barely scraping by, depending on others for survival. A husband's model is Jesus Christ who desires prosperity for us, soul and spirit. He desires his wife's physical well-being above his own.

Honor

The marriage vow promises that a husband will "love, honor and keep" his wife, and the Bible commands that a wife respect her husband.

Before the Fall there was no conflict between man and woman. Only when sin entered the world did the degradation of abuse infect the marriage relationship. Dishonor began when Adam tried to lay all the blame for the Fall on his wife, a misogynistic trait; while honor recognizes a spouse's equal position. See Paul's statement in 1 Corinthians 15:22, "as in Adam all die."

Peter told Christian husbands to grant their wives "honor as a fellow heir of the grace of life" (1 Peter 3:7). It was a sharp departure from the way Jewish men treated their wives, which was according to the man-decreed injunctions of the Talmud. To the rabbis who wrote these, women were pieces of property.

But Paul exhorts Christian men to love their wives with the love of Christ, that God "raised us up *with* Him, and seated us *with* Him in the heavenly places" (Ephesians 2:6, italics mine). It is the Lord's desire to share His position of honor with His Bride, the Church.

Communication

When communication ceases, a marriage deteriorates. As the commitment becomes more and more one-sided, any attempt to nourish the relationship by expressing thoughts, ideas and love gradually fades. Often one spouse adopts a passive-aggressive role, refusing to communicate, manipulating the other through his or her silence. The other spouse makes all the attempts to reconcile, comply, soothe and nourish the relationship with little cooperation.

Commitment

To sustain a marriage, there must be mutual commitment. Marriage by very definition involves two, not one. When one spouse no longer wants to remain married, the commitment dissolves. Commitment is evidenced by action; a dead relationship is motionless.

When a woman becomes a victim of abuse, the elements of a real marriage are gradually erased until the bond no longer exists. Two people may be held together by a piece of paper, living together under the same roof, but the true state of the relationship before God is emotional, spiritual and physical divorce.

When a marriage loses any one of the elements above, it reflects less of the glory of Christ and the Church and gradually becomes a playground for Satan.

Still, marriage was God's invention and is not to be subject to man's perversion. It was instituted to reflect not Satan and his victims but Jesus Christ and the Church; while misogyny thrives on ignorance of Scripture and of the nature of godly boundaries.

God has even set boundaries by which we may enter His presence. He spoke through Isaiah:

> "I permitted Myself to be sought by those who did not ask for Me; I permitted Myself to be found by those who did not seek Me. I said, 'Here am I, here am I,' to a nation which did not call on My name. I have spread out My hands all day long to a

rebellious people, who walk in the way which is not good, following their own thoughts."

Isaiah 65:1–2

When God extended Himself to the nation of Israel as an example of His desire to show mercy to all nations, He was repeatedly rejected and abused. Instead of committing Himself to nations, He now commits Himself to individuals. He has established a boundary of holiness and righteousness about Himself, but has left open a door of grace. That Door, the Lord Jesus Christ, is the only way to find God, who commands all the respect and admiration of Father and Friend.

The Journey Out

It was Bud, surprisingly, who inadvertently helped Wendy turn to boundaries in her life. At his insistence that they move on to yet another church, Wendy met a pastor who could reach her with the truth. Her heart was still tender toward God after all she had suffered, and she was finally able to believe that her heavenly Father was not like her earthly father. He did not want her to suffer abuse. Through counseling Wendy started on her journey out of codependency, and she began by circumscribing boundaries.

When Wendy discovered that a real Christian marriage contained all the elements above and that they were her spiritual heritage in Christ, she began to insist on them. She lay Bud at Jesus' feet and placed her earlier "need" to be married to an abuser on the altar.

When she saw she was actually perpetuating Bud's immoral, abusive behavior by not setting boundaries, Wendy began to refuse Bud's abuse. Moving slowly but with a new understanding of Jesus' love, and realizing she was not responsible for his actions, she began to set limits on what she would take. At the advice of her counselor she left Bud a door of grace: If he would submit to counseling and implement change, she would agree to continue living with him. If not, he could find another victim.

When he tried to make her leave their current church, she said, "No way!" When he tried to isolate her from her new friends, she would not give in. When he demanded that she submit to perverse sexual acts, she changed bedrooms. When he abused her verbally and refused to apologize, she warned him. And when he continued to shove her around, she followed her pastor's advice and moved out.

There is no doubt that Wendy's life was beginning to be endangered. The pattern of domestic violence begins, according to statistics issued by the U. S. Department of Justice and reported in the December 12, 1988, issue of *Newsweek,* with milder manifestations such as shoving, pushing, grabbing the neck, arms or head, and escalating to blows, kicks, more violent forms of manhandling and the use of weapons. Before the woman is aware that her life is on the line, it may be too late. Some form of violence, moreover, is happening in one out of every four marriages.

Wendy was right in leaving. But, amazingly, some of her friends criticized her, telling her that a Christian wife should suffer abuse and degradation with the hope of saving her husband. Let's look more closely at why this is not a biblical stance.

Stay with an Unbeliever?

In 1 Corinthians 7:10-16 Paul exhorts husbands and wives not to leave their unbelieving spouses *if those spouses are willing to dwell with them in peace.* We might say that a Christian wife establishes the borders, based on her walk with Christ, of what she will allow in her life. Otherwise, what reason would an unbelieving husband have to leave if his perverse acts were never challenged by godly boundaries?

"God has called us to peace," wrote Paul (verse 15). I infer from this that peace is more important than sacrifice in the slim hope that the spouse will accept Christ.

We may have heard stories of women who suffered lives of torture and whose husbands prayed the sinner's prayer on their deathbeds. These words of Peter may have been held up as proof that it was her sacrifice that saved him: "You wives, be submissive to your own husbands so that even if any of them are disobedient to the word, they may be won without a word by the behavior of their wives, as they observe your chaste and respectful behavior" (1 Peter 3:1-2).

Please understand: Peter was not exhorting the Christian wife to suffer abuse to save her husband, but rather to trust in the power of God alone—and not her own nagging, for example, or her own strength—to save her husband. Who knows how much sooner an unbelieving husband might have recognized his need for salvation if godly boundaries had been placed in his path?

Every woman has a right to be at rest in her home—not only from attack, but from feeling she has to browbeat her husband to Christ. If he is to be won, it can be accomplished quietly, by the Holy Spirit's power, as she commits the matter to Him. If her husband is to be converted, it is his belief in the atonement of Christ—and not his wife's sacrifice—that saves him. Otherwise, she could take the credit for it.

It is also clear that Peter was not advocating that wives submit to the abuse of their husbands from his admonition to husbands a few verses later: "You husbands likewise, live with your wives in an understanding way, as with a weaker vessel, since she is a woman; and grant her honor . . . " (verse 7). Peter even warned the husband that his prayers would be hindered if he did not show his wife understanding and honor.

Further scriptural guidance to abused wives—should they stay and submit to the abuse?—is given in the example of the Lord Jesus Christ. He laid down His life at Calvary; no man took it from Him. But on two occasions Jesus so offended the theology of the scribes and Pharisees that they picked up stones to stone Him to death. Each time, the Scripture says, "Jesus hid Himself" and "eluded their grasp" (John 8:59, 10:39). He would not allow Himself to be needlessly abused.

On another occasion Jesus told His followers, "Be sure of this, that if the head of the house had known at what time of the night the thief was coming, he would have been on the alert and would not have allowed his house to be broken into" (Matthew 24:43).

As we grow closer to the time of Jesus' return, violence and lawlessness will increase, as He promised, and love will grow cold. In order to conduct ourselves properly in such a time, we must take measures to prevent needless victimization. This is only sensible, and most women do this automatically. The codependent, by contrast, is never in control of how and when she lays down her life for the cause of Christ. She is putting her life in the hands of someone else besides her Savior.

When you know it is not God's time to lay yourself at the feet of untimely persecution, do what Jesus did: Hide yourself. Elude your abuser's grasp. Perhaps the safest places are the shelters for abused women in your area, which can be found by phoning the police, hotlines or social agencies in the phone book. Phone calls may be made anonymously and each shelter is committed to your privacy.

Shelters provide counsel, a safe place to protect your children, gain your bearings and find a place to live. Before making such a move, investigate the shelters in your area. Find out how long you may stay at a shelter and how long it takes to receive your first benefits after signing up for temporary public assistance for women in your situation. (Make sure your time at the shelter does not run out before the check comes.)

Investigate your legal options by contacting an attorney who will protect your rights in such matters. This is no time for passive legal counsel, particularly if your children's welfare is at stake.

Whatever you do, once you have escaped your abusive environment, do not return. The pattern of abused women is to suffer remorse and return to the abuser (just as an alcoholic returns to drink), unable to adjust emotionally to life without violence. Unless your husband follows through with extensive professional counseling and implements long-term change, resolve to stand your ground and insist on the boundaries you have established. If you return to the abuse, all gains made by the separation will prove ineffective. Your husband will return to his old patterns and who knows the next time whether or not you will escape?

Be aware, furthermore, that when physical conflict erupts between husband and wife, and that conflict ends in the husband's accidental death, the wife in most states may be charged with and convicted of homicide. All documented past evidence of his abuse is not even permitted as evidence in a court of law. In a recent segment of ABC's *20/20*, Lynn Sherr interviewed victims of domestic violence serving fifteen years to life in an Arizona prison. Women who look like your sister and grandmother, victims of repeated domestic violence, are all victims of this legal loophole.

A pastor's wife from another community told me that several years ago the elders in her church counseled a woman being abused by her husband. They advised her to remain with him and hope patiently for his salvation. He killed her. That pastor's wife told me she hopes the family never discovers the kind of counsel the woman received from those well-meaning brethren!

Today Wendy and Bud are in counseling. It remains to be seen whether the marriage will be restored. Meanwhile, Wendy is in secretarial school preparing to stand on her own with God's help if Bud will not change. Wendy has learned that spiritual warfare means resisting the devil's stealthy invasion and seeing him flee. Sometimes it is necessary to cast the man as well as the demon out if the two cannot be separated.

When Boundaries Work

Can establishing godly boundaries ever work to revive a marriage? Several months ago, when my husband and I were guests on a radio talk show, a woman I will call Sheila phoned in. A few weeks later she brought her husband, Jesse, with her to counsel with Bill and me.

Jesse's life paralleled Bud Milford's so closely, he could have been his brother. Divorced twice before, Jesse had experienced the pain of abandonment, which had precipitated his misogynistic treatment of Sheila. They were on the brink of divorce. Both Sheila and Jesse sat, hardened and bitter, across the table.

As Bill and I listened, Jesse chronicled how he had abused and dominated his wife. He described his certain conviction that his views were scriptural. He did not feel that counseling was biblical. But Sheila was giving counseling one last try. Their faces were mirror images of the darkness I remembered on Bud and Wendy Milford's faces. But something wonderful was to happen to Jesse and Sheila.

Bill spoke words of sound advice to Jesse and loaned him a set of Christian videos on how to have a loving relationship. We gave Jesse a copy of my first book, *When Addiction Comes to Church*, which Jesse agreed reluctantly to read. After they left our office, Bill and I agreed that nothing short of a miracle would save the marriage.

A little over three weeks later, Sheila called to make another counseling appointment. We sat amazed as she told us about those three weeks. As Jesse had watched the videos and read the book, his denial over his compulsive/addictive behavior had begun to crack. His heart began to melt. Jesse realized that dysfunctional behavior and a fear of abandonment had caused him to trap Sheila in a cage—a cage from which he had now decided to set her free.

He began by apologizing to his wife and restoring communication, which had all but ceased. Sheila was suspicious, but took heart when Jesse stood up before the men's prayer breakfast at church and confessed his addictive behavior and mistreatment of her. He asked for public forgiveness and exhorted the other men, especially those struggling with addictions, to study the materials he had.

This was only the beginning. During the ensuing weeks, he realized how mean he had been to the counselor before us who had tried so desperately to help him and Sheila. He phoned the counselor and apologized.

Several times during the next few months, Jesse and Sheila had disagreements that erupted into arguments. But Sheila confessed to Bill and me her amazement when Jesse stopped in the middle and acknowledged that his reactions were the result of his old behaviors and dysfunctional upbringing. He apologized for hurting her and for not listening. And the issues resolved themselves without verbal and physical abuse.

Jesse and Sheila are still in counseling, but their hardened hearts are melted. Their countenances shine. Jesse told Bill and me, "The Lord has released me from having to play God. I realize now that anything Sheila is doing for the Lord—well, it's the same as if I were doing it. I don't have to compete with her. She's part of me!"

Was the success a result of expert counseling? I doubt it. We have given the same counsel to others who did not respond. The difference was Jesse's willingness to hear the truth, humble himself and change. There are still many issues he and Sheila need to face, but those trials will more than likely fall like dominoes, because in place of rebellious resistance is teachability and humility.

We cannot help but wonder what would have happened if Wendy and Sheila had not set boundaries and enforced them. All too many Christian women never do. What keeps them victims?

Let's examine next the binding power of self-sabotage.

6

. . . .

Submission or Self-Sabotage?

When a Christian woman is asked repeatedly to sacrifice one or more of the elements that make a real marriage, it is not long before she feels used. Her boundaries are being violated, which will result ultimately in some form of rage.

For Jennifer, the roller coaster ride to despair involved a mishmash of serious problems. She turned to a coping mechanism many women employ to get even—a coping mechanism that was destroying her.

The Controlling Husband

To this day Jennifer is not sure why she freezes emotionally whenever her father or another man walks into a room with her alone. She has no conscious memories of sexual molestation, but she does show emotional scars from it. These scars helped form her primary stressor, which set her up for spiritual abuse.

Jennifer had several love disappointments in high school and one broken engagement in college. By the time she was in her early twenties, she was seeing a counselor. Although she was intelligent and attractive, her self-esteem was low; and although she was efficient in her government job, she had bouts of self-doubt about major decisions in life.

Then, in her late twenties, Jennifer met Bob at a prayer meeting. Bob had come to the Lord recently and was already an elder in their church. He was also the most zealous and intelligent man she had ever met. Although there were many other single women at church that Jennifer felt he would be more attracted to, Bob started showing an interest in her.

After dating her only a week, Bob proposed marriage. "The Lord told me that I should ask you to marry me," he said. Jennifer was astounded that someone as spiritual as Bob would choose her and she agreed readily. They set the wedding date for a few weeks away. It seemed that her life was finally taking a turn toward real happiness.

In the next few weeks Jennifer and Bob got caught up in a whirlwind of preparations that masked the subtle appearance of several serious conflicts. Sure enough, a few days after their wedding Jennifer was angry at her husband. Bob was affectionate, but he had several expectations Jennifer found hard to live with.

For one thing, Bob did not believe in birth control. He saw it as unscriptural and felt that a Christian couple should have as many children as possible. "Be fruitful and multiply" was the verse he quoted. Jennifer wanted to keep her job and wait to get their marriage on firm footing, but Bob insisted they start a family *now*.

Jennifer was also uncomfortable with the way Bob wanted her to look. He seemed convinced that a Christian woman should not dress in any way that might attract men. He firmly insisted that Jennifer, who had always dressed tastefully, opt for "simpler" clothes, as he put it. He wanted no bright colors, no cosmetics or perfume, not even any deodorant.

Bob believed further that, according to the Scriptures, women should keep their hair long since it was their covering. Full of self-doubt already, but believing she should submit to her husband's authority, Jennifer complied—but it wasn't long before she hated how she looked. Still, she was afraid to question Bob's decisions. After all, the husband, she knew from the Bible, has "power over the wife's body."

Bob had been brought up by alcoholic parents who spent little time with him. He had early been forced to learn to meet his own emotional needs and had thus become highly self-sufficient. Perhaps this bothered Jennifer more than anything. Bob paid lipservice to his need for her, but his actions said all too loudly, "I can do without you."

Bob's lack of good parental role models left him unclear about what family life should be like. In his attempt—like that of many adult children of alcoholics—to discover what "normal" was, Bob thought he saw that missing role model in the words of Scripture. The problem was, he saw only one way in the Scriptures, his way. Blinded to the tremendous latitude afforded in the Bible on many issues, Bob chided Jennifer and questioned her spirituality whenever they disagreed.

And Jennifer felt guilty for disagreeing. *After all,* she would think, *Bob must know what's right; he's an elder in the church.* She submitted to him in everything.

Six years later, five small children were crying and playing at Jennifer's feet. Bob was oblivious to the strain the children placed on her, believing that, since it was a woman's calling to bear children, God would give her the grace to be happy and content in her home. He was proud of his five children, but had little idea how to control them.

Bob's position in the church added more pressure. Jennifer was frequently left alone with the children while Bob, extremely active as an elder, was out ministering to needs in the congregation. With her self-doubt, Jennifer found it hard to know how to set boundaries for her children—what to permit and when to punish. When Jennifer and Bob were home together, Bob would ignore the children, shutting off the noise around him, and take a hand only when Jennifer had had enough. The children sensed disagreement between their parents over discipline and manipulated the home scene with all the cunning of a platoon of well-trained troops.

Because it was hard to find a babysitter for five difficult children, Jennifer felt trapped in her home. Rather than the pleasant retreat it should have been, it afforded only chaos. By her early thirties Jennifer felt like "a baby factory." And when she did get out, she had little freedom since the checking account was in Bob's name only. She did not feel free to express her feelings for fear of spiritual chastisement from him.

Jennifer felt especially guilty when she or one of the children needed to go to the doctor. Bob always made her feel as though her faith were deficient. Besides, he did not want to waste money on doctors that could go to missions. They had no insurance because their church considered that a lack of faith, even though others in the church would break down, show their faith was weak, shame themselves and seek medical attention.

For all these reasons Jennifer, under increasing physical stress, let many symptoms go ignored; but when she started hemorrhaging she finally had to tell Bob. When prayers did not stop the bleeding, Bob agreed reluctantly to let her visit the doctor, though he could not bring himself to go with her. Jennifer learned that she faced an immediate hysterectomy—multi-thousand-dollar uninsured surgery—with the possibility of the presence of cancer, all without the emotional support of her husband.

The years were driving them apart. There was little communication without tempers flaring. Jennifer often felt rage, but because she was expected to be spiritual, could not express it. She bottled it up and stored it on a shelf, until one day all the bottles were full. That was when Jennifer developed skill in deploying her only remaining weapon.

The Weapon of Self-Sabotage

When a woman like Jennifer has no other outlet for anger, she may turn to the only weapon she has left in her arsenal, self-sabotage.

Bob could see that Jennifer's stress-filled life was taking a physical toll. But it seemed to him that, after her lapse of faith and resultant hysterectomy (no cancer), Jennifer was becoming afraid of every sniffle. She was always sick. Whenever he was out ministering, it seemed, a phone call would interrupt him. Her pitiful voice would whine, "My back is killing me. How much longer will you be? The kids won't go to bed. . . . "

Sometimes Jennifer would lie in bed for several days and her oldest daughter, age eight, would find clothes for the other children, make their breakfasts and fix the sack lunches. Sometimes Bob was forced to suspend activities at church and cancel meetings so he could look after his wife. Because he did not want to take Jennifer to the doctor—it would be an indication of spiritual failure—Bob often made excuses at the church office.

From her standpoint, Jennifer enjoyed the attention she received when she was ill. In fact, it was her main source of attention and she was determined that no one would take it from her. It seemed to people she knew that she was magnifying her illnesses beyond proportion, but they played along anyhow.

When Jennifer was not sick, she found attention in other ways. She had never gotten a driver's license and now refused stubbornly to get one. She asked her friends to take her to appointments and to the store. One by one her friends grew tired of her dependency and the tactic she thought would be a lifeline to the outside world.

Although Jennifer's dependency had pleased Bob at first, he began to tire of her whimpering and passivity. He was also growing angry. Whenever he lost his temper he raised his voice, but Jennifer only grew weaker. Bob began to drop hints around others who were "spiritual" that his wife needed prayer. It was a way to let others know he was suffering under the weight of a spiritually weak wife.

By the time Jennifer reached her early forties, the kids were growing more independent. She herself, by contrast, had become so dependent on others that functioning without their codependency was impossible. She resented them and was filled with contempt for herself. She criticized other women stronger than she and resisted their attempts to encourage her to leave her cocoon. Jennifer was caught in squirrel-cage existence, lost in the isolating cycle of self-sabotage.

What Is Self-Sabotage?

A woman commits self-sabotage when she hurts herself to retaliate against others to whom she is reluctant to show anger. Self-sabotage may begin with a woman's failure to believe in herself and her worth before the Lord. It may take the form of a simple refusal to act on her own behalf, and it may escalate to more severe passive-aggressive actions. Anything from silent withdrawal and pouting to acts that contain the element of spite toward self—quitting a job, over- or undereating, refusing an open door of opportunity, even verbal self-abuse—are all manifestations of this emotionally destructive weapon.

A woman afraid of showing anger is not the only one to employ the technique of self-sabotage. It may also be used by a woman whose repeated expressions of anger do little to change her husband or even win his ear. Self-sabotage is frequently the weapon of a woman victimized by a more aggressive person or by passive-aggressive behavior in others.

Self-sabotage is, at its heart, a substitute for influence. It is the determination to have a say in life, even if the only way is to manipulate.

When a husband takes a wife, he should honor her by giving her the right of influence in his life. Because he has ultimate authority in the home, he must take the responsibility for the decisions made. (More on this in a minute.) But he is a foolish man who does not choose a wife whose influence he respects.

One root of self-sabotage, then, is *misunderstanding the difference between authority and influence.* Isaac's wife, Rebekah, lived in a time when men had absolute authority over their wives. Women were little more than pieces of property. So in order to help her favored son, Jacob, obtain the blessing that belonged by rights to Esau, she felt she had to resort to aggressive manipulation.

The godly influence of Queen Esther, by contrast, saved her people, but her influence came at the risk of her own life. It is interesting that Ahasuerus, king of the Medes and Persians, allowed Esther to influence him. Had he not, he would have been manipulated by the wicked Haman to commit genocide against the Jews in his kingdom.

A woman committed to self-sabotage has, unlike Esther, lost her willingness to risk in a relationship. Perhaps this is due to the humiliation of verbal abuse, her unwillingness to risk the "peace-at-any-price" status quo, even the terror of physical abuse. But in order to break out of passivity she must be willing to risk these, and perhaps the relationship itself, for godly change to take place.

Women like Esther will understand what is at stake and take the risk. Possessing the right of influence is vital to a wife's enjoyment of the marriage relationship.

Another root of self-sabotage is *the feeling of victimization that comes from feeling forced by God into a relationship*. Jennifer married Bob on the basis of the "word from God" Bob said he received. From a pastoral standpoint, I must say that every marriage Bill and I know of that began on this footing is ridden with conflict. The parties spend lifetimes trying to reconcile their own feelings and their God-given right to choose while the so-called "will of God" is imposed in the name of obedience or spirituality.

God will offer anyone guidance in the selection of a mate, but the responsibility for the decision rests with the individual. It is important to subtract the added pressure of "the will of God" from one another.

The Cycle of Self-Sabotage

The cycle of self-sabotage begins with vulnerability created by the presence of a primary stressor. Jennifer's early wounds and subsequent insecurities made her a compliant target for spiritual abuse. Anger accumulated until part of Jennifer hated her husband and her own role in the home, which was little more than that of an older child. When her anger went unresolved, Jennifer sought to get even with Bob by further destroying herself, compounding her self-contempt.

The sabotage itself followed without challenge as she subconsciously yet willfully cut herself off from anything that would edify her or lift her self-esteem. Her self-sabotage was designed not only to destroy herself, whom she had come to hate, but to manipulate Bob, who had come to see himself as the victim. His anger only produced more emotional abuse and perpetuated the cycle.

Since Bob and Jennifer have played the roles of manipulator and victim interchangeably for so long, it is difficult to determine who is more at fault for this dysfunctional family model. Their friends are mystified as to how to bring real or lasting help. Though the Lord continues to use Bob, Jennifer feels useless to God and to her children, who have all but outgrown their dependence on her as they try to function as adults—a realm she has not lived in for years.

She feels most useless to her husband, of course, and spends the biggest part of her time wishing she were somewhere else. Thoughts of suicide, the ultimate form of self-sabotage, have occurred to her more than once as she fantasizes the only way out of her misery. The shame of divorce would be too great.

Jennifer has pled with Bob to go with her for counseling, but Bob refuses, deeming it unspiritual. He holds up his spiritual successes as signs that God is vindicating and blessing his life. He is willing only to take their problem before the men of the church, who he knows will tell Jennifer to comply with scriptural admonitions and submit.

And he now hints about Jennifer's lack of spirituality in front of the children.

The girls are angry with her for not standing up to their father. The boys are developing a negative attitude about women that will set them up to repeat the dysfunctional pattern in their own homes.

Breaking Denial

Early in their marriage Bob's ignorance of how to treat a woman, coupled with his narrow interpretation of Scripture, caused him to make several serious mistakes in his relationship with Jennifer. By requiring Jennifer to submit to his own legalistic standards of holiness, he took from her the right to hear her own conscience and the voice of God for herself. By chiding her and reminding her constantly how she ought to be feeling as a Christian, he taught her to stuff her anger inside. He forced a lifestyle on her that robbed her of the freedom to choose.

Without realizing it, Bob robbed his wife of one of the primary ingredients of a marriage, the honor of being treated as an equal. He fancies himself a model Christian husband, having done everything that he feels should produce results. But because he believes deep down that Jennifer is not his equal, he has never considered her feelings. Although he protests he does, his actions speak a different message—one that is demeaning to women. All his attention toward Jennifer and their home has been aimed at absolving his own conscience rather than developing communication and intimacy with his wife. Intimacy might require experiencing and sharing feelings and this he fears.

Just as an addict needs to break denial to interrupt the destructive cycle of addiction, Bob (and men like him) need to break denial, too. Once they stop denying there is a problem, they must take a closer look at the Bible from a perspective they have been unable (if not unwilling) to see. It is the only way change will occur.

The Alternative: Godly Submission

I have already quoted 1 Peter 3:7, in which Peter says how to treat Christian wives: "Live with your wives in an understanding way, as with a weaker vessel, since she is a woman."

For centuries this verse has been misconstrued by Christians to mean that women are inferior, while Peter is actually saying the opposite. Treat your wife, he says, not like a plastic cup but like a fragile crystal goblet. The goblet occupies a place of honor. It is exhibited in elegance for all to see. It is to be treated gently and with respect.

But how many men treat their wives as little better than a plastic cup, inferior in value? Instead of being lifted up, they are put down. They are treated as common, ordinary things to be used and tossed out or hidden away and forgotten until the next time their services are needed.

A woman who sees herself as a plastic cup cooperates because, after all, she must deserve it. God must expect her to submit to such treatment. All the while, something inside her longs for the place of honor and respect.

How many Christian men believe they are loving their wives when they do not bother to understand them, to validate their feelings, to reinforce their right to a differing opinion (which may be closer to the will of God than their own)? How many Christian husbands cut themselves off by not receiving a wife's perspective, counsel or wisdom? How many quench the Holy Spirit in their wives by not making their wives' spiritual well-being their chief concern?

Husbands can learn a lot from the attitude of God Himself. Never does God prey on a person's vulnerability, even to achieve His own redemptive purpose. God never forces Himself on anyone. Rather, with all restraint, He respects the independent will He created in human beings.

One of the most beautiful examples of God's restraint is seen in His dealings with Mary, the mother of Jesus. Before He used Mary's virginity, He sent His chief angel to "ask permission." He revealed to her His plan, which He had concealed from every other human being on the earth. He was looking for receptivity in her. This is the Lord's secret of having joyful servants: We can decide *not* to go along, a choice which gives us the freedom to say yes. Mary replied to Gabriel, "Behold, the bondslave of the Lord; be it done to me according to your word" (Luke 1:38). She found joy in cooperating with God in the ultimate blessed event.

In the same way, Jesus' chief concern is our spiritual welfare. He died, rose and is seated at the right hand of the Father, and He wants to raise His Bride, the Church, to be seated with Him—not below Him—in heavenly places. And our response to His desire to honor us is also the secret of a wife's submission.

The Secret of Submission

We worship and honor the One who gave His life to make us like Him, to share with us His place of honor. The Christian man who treats his wife as Christ treats the Church will find not a resentful slave but a willing partner.

The Greek word Paul used for submission, *hupotasso*, actually means "to rank under, fit into, harmonize with." Dwelling in harmony implies agreement. And where there is agreement, there is no need for submission.

In choosing a mate for life, it is of supreme importance to choose one with whom you agree on almost all important issues. Only occasionally should a woman be faced with the dilemma of having to surrender her opinion in the interest of "ranking under" her husband. And when that happens, conformity should not be forced before she has an opportunity to express her wisdom and concern.

The concept of a wife's submission was not invented, as some have suggested, to keep the easily deceived woman under wraps. Nor was it imposed by God as a punishment for Eve after the Fall. Nor was it to be imposed on every woman, single or married. Submission fits only into the context of marriage, in which someone must make the final decision.

When God told Eve that "your desire shall be for your husband, and he shall rule over you" (Genesis 3:16), the tense of the verb is actually *will rule*, which implies statement of fact, not *shall rule*, which implies command. This verb tense reveals that God was prophesying that woman would be dominated by fallen man given to hardness of heart and the fear-induced need to control.

In fact, the verse is translated differently (and more correctly) in the Septuagint, the Greek translation of the Old Testament used during Paul's time by Jewish synagogues and by early Christian churches whose members spoke Greek. It renders it: "You are turning away to your husband and he will dominate you." Adam's God-given mandate and desire to subdue the earth would be perverted by sin and turned on woman. Woman's natural physical weakness would magnify this tendency.

In Christian marriage, a woman is restored to her pre-Fall position in Christ where there is equality not only of position but of responsibility. Her calling to help man is fulfilled if she is given the freedom to do so, not only by bearing children but by bearing spiritual fruit, by fitting in with God's divine purpose to multiply and subdue the earth for God's Kingdom.

Submission in marriage was designed to release a woman, to define her boundaries of authority and responsibility, not to dominate or subdue her. Submission was never intended as a means whereby the greater will of God could be subjugated to a man's or woman's tyrannical will. In no case is domination a Christian value. Being "subject to one another in the fear of Christ" (Ephesians 5:21) causes both parties to look for the greater will of God instead of engaging themselves in a power struggle.

Submission enables a couple to move forward at an impasse. Its purpose is to free the marriage from occasional stalemate. It frees the husband to be wrong and to discover it by running into God's greater will. And sometimes, a few steps down the road as the wife is called on to subordinate her opinion to that of her husband, he finds out he is mistaken and seeks to rectify the mistake—a point that would never be reached were there no submission, for the relationship would be locked in conflict.

Two examples from the Old Testament stand out in which God blessed a wife's opinion over that of her husband. First, an intelligent and beautiful woman named Abigail showed hospitality to David and his men after her husband, Nabal, had brutishly turned them away (1 Samuel 25). In so doing she saved all the males in her household from slaughter. "Blessed be your discernment," said David, "and blessed be you" (verse 33).

When Abraham was afraid to send Ishmael and Hagar away as Sarah had requested, God spoke out of heaven telling Abraham to listen to his wife. She was right. Her opinion was God's at a time when sentimentality blinded Abraham's eyes to the truth. Sarah's word to Abraham—"Cast out the bond-woman and her son, for the son of the bondwoman shall not be an heir with the son of the free woman" (Galatians 4:30; see Genesis 21:10, 12)—became the New Testament picture of the two covenants, one of Law, one of the promise of the Spirit.

Learning to walk in harmony with God and his wife was not always easy, even for a patriarch like Abraham!

Any husband and wife can learn to harmonize, however, if both are submitted to God. Two submissive people will find it easy to learn to harmonize. A courtship ridden with conflict, on the other hand, is a clue that the relationship will not make a harmonious marriage.

A woman who feels she must sacrifice her self-esteem, her calling from God or her most valued opinions on the altar of a relationship will never truly be happy or have her personal worth affirmed. Paul called husbands and wives to peace (1 Corinthians 7:15), but not at any price. As precious as the marriage bond is in the sight of God, the Lordship of Christ is preeminent. No one should ever be asked, for whatever reason, to become someone he or she is not.

Can the Cycle Be Broken?

Can a woman like Jennifer learn to practice true submission after so many destructive years? Breaking the cycle of self-sabotage requires that she recover ground that has been lost. Jennifer's loss began when she allowed her husband's legalistic injunctions to take away her right to listen to her own conscience. In order to take back that ground, a woman must *begin to act according to her own conscience before God.*

The conscience given by God to every human being was programmed to react whenever the individual exceeds God's boundaries and commits sin. The conscience is also programmed by parental teaching or the lack of it. It responds to the traditions a person has grown up with or been impressed by. Religious tradition—man's law, not God's—has the power to control and sometimes abuse the conscience, while the Holy Spirit reserves the right to sensitize the conscience not only to the letter of the law, but to the Spirit.

Many Christians from hurting homes are taught, through dysfunctional rigidity, to ignore God-given promptings in the interest of preserving what seems legally right. The properly activated conscience responds not out of rigidity or dysfunctional fears, but wisdom. The Christian's conscience when touched by the Holy Spirit has the power to recreate him or her into the person God the Father intends.

For this reason we must respect the consciences of others and allow them to conduct their lives according to how they believe God is leading them. Violating the conscience of another interferes with that individual's developing ability to hear from God himself, to find God's will for him. Giving an individual the freedom to choose according to his conscience allows him to mature spiritually. Think of a chick being strengthened by pecking its way out of the enveloping egg. So is a Christian, free to hear from God, enabled to live outside immature, restrictive boundaries.

Jennifer also lost ground and assisted the cycle of self-sabotage when she surrendered her personal boundaries to Bob. We observed in the last chapter that all warfare, natural and spiritual, is conducted over boundaries. Jennifer allowed Bob to redefine and shrink the borders of her life: Start a family immediately, forget about birth control, quit your job, stay at home.

Every Christian is entitled to righteous, fair boundaries. So a second step in breaking the cycle of self-sabotage is for a woman to *find out, with God's help, what the borders of her life should be, and then guard those borders*.

For the younger wife caught in the cycle of self-sabotage, birth control is not an option; it is a necessity. It is part of setting boundaries for a woman's emotional well-being and that of the children she may already have. Child abuse, moreover, is often a result of an angry mother trapped in a cycle of self-sabotage.

Let me be quick to add that a woman's choice exists before conception, not after. A mother whose "quiver is full," who has more olive plants around her garden than she can successfully nourish and prune, has every right to consider a temporary (or perhaps permanent) method of birth control. The husband who values his relationship with her will agree. If he does not, or if he prizes her only for her productive womb, he is likely to have a wife committed to getting even through self-sabotage.

Once children are here, learning to love and discipline them is of primary importance in achieving peace in the home. There is a wealth of good Christian books to help mothers establish and enforce boundaries for their children and guide them to maturity.

Cathy's Story

After I taught a seminar on the subject of boundaries in a Christian woman's life, a woman named Cathy stood to give her testimony. The positive outcome illustrates the principle of boundary-setting in the face of an unbelieving husband's will.

Cathy had become a Christian some time before, and was turning into a woman her husband, Richard, didn't like. She was losing interest in sensual forms of entertainment they had previously enjoyed together. Nor was she available to take off with him every weekend, since now she wanted to go to church.

So Richard forbade Cathy to go to church, hoping her newfound faith would wither and die if she was severed from fellowship with like-minded people. He appeared ready to enforce his injunction with mean, dictatorial behavior.

Cathy loved her husband, but she loved God more. Giving up church attendance was something her conscience would not allow. So she informed her husband that although she loved him very much, she wanted to go to church and was committed to developing her spiritual life.

In responding this way, Cathy was instituting a boundary in her life to preserve her relationship with God—the most important relationship anyone has. She clung to this verse: "Not forsaking our own assembling together, as is the habit of some, but encouraging one another; and all the more, as you see the day drawing near" (Hebrews 10:25).

Cathy's husband was not happy. But her establishment of this boundary and preserving it at the risk of losing him resulted in his eventual salvation. Within a few months he decided to go to church with her because he wanted to learn "what this is all about." He came under the conviction of sin and accepted Christ.

What happened with Cathy's husband does not happen every time. Not every husband finds salvation through his wife's determination of boundaries. Sometimes, in fact, a wife's new resolve means that she loses her husband's affection. For those cases—though this is a hard saying—the Word of God says, "If the unbelieving one leaves, let him leave" (1 Corinthians 7:15).

Most of the time, however, unbelieving husbands grow to respect their wives for showing strength of conviction. In the case of "a woman who has an unbelieving husband," advises the apostle Paul, "and he consents to live with her [implying that they live within godly boundaries], let her not send her husband away" (1 Corinthians 7:13). Taking the risk of setting boundaries involves dying to the part of you that wants to remain passive.

Jennifer has not yet developed the strength to take her stand and define her boundaries. She lives in passivity and still substitutes self-sabotage for godly submission. Women in her situation have been deceived into giving every inch of ground to Satan, who is working against them through the closest relationship in their lives. He deprives them of self-worth, of the right to hear from God, and he paralyzes them into destructive passivity.

The healthy Christian woman, on the other hand, learns to draw her boundaries, walk in godly submission with her mate and find peace in her relationships. She knows the joy of being loved and respected by her husband and children for the woman of excellence God created her to be.

Now let's look at a woman whose internal pain came from a different kind of husband-wife relationship—the opposite of Bob and Jennifer's—and see how she discovered through her problem the secret of true intimacy with her husband.

7

●●●●●●●●●●●●●●●●●●●●●●●●

The Secret of Intimacy

When a woman marries, she hopes to find a measure of rest in her husband's arms. She carries with her from birth the dependency needs common to all members of the human race: the need for love, acceptance, provision. Finding in her mate the fulfillment of these needs brings her to a place of rest not unlike the Sabbath rest a believer finds in the arms of our heavenly Father.

Part of a woman's search for the right mate may depend on her relationship with her earthly father. It is a universally accepted proverb that a woman usually marries a man like her father or the father she missed.

Eileen was looking for all these needs to be filled when she met and married Eddie.

Eileen and Eddie

They met in law school and seemed made for each other.

Leaving the shame of her alcoholic home far behind, Eileen had packed her bags and headed for college under a scholarship she had fought hard to win. She had sailed through undergraduate school with few hurdles. In law school, though, she had found herself surrounded by highly competitive, insensitive men who enjoyed the challenge of winning debates against a female attorney a little more than they should have.

Eileen's mother regretted marrying her father, nagged him constantly and sometimes warned Eileen that the same might happen to her if she were not careful. "Never marry the first thing that comes along," her mother advised her. "Make sure you have a career in place—something to fall back on if you do get married. You just never know what might happen."

Eileen was determined not to wind up like her mother or the girls in high school who were housewives by the time they were nineteen. Intelligence, coupled with the driving ambition to make something of herself, propelled Eileen to graduate cum laude from law school and begin working in a firm near the campus.

Eddie's story was different. His mother was shy. His father, bold and aggressive, was a traveling salesman whose home office transferred him frequently. Eddie grew up without roots, afraid to make friends for fear of losing them at the capricious decision of his dad's company. Eddie never wanted to be victimized by a company again and entered law school hoping to remain his own boss the rest of his life.

Eddie was not like the hard-driving attorneys Eileen had come to dislike. He was a quiet, gentle man whose poise she appreciated. Though she was talkative and spontaneous, Eddie was reserved and slower to jump into uncharted territory. Eileen felt this was a good balance for her; his cautiousness would prevent catastrophic conflicts with others. And he told her how he appreciated her ability to break the ice with new people. Once Eileen initiated a conversation, Eddie could enter in and engage in witty repartee. She saw in him the good qualities her father had possessed without the alcoholism that had corrupted him. Eddie loved her and wanted to date no one else.

Eileen's ability to make friends quickly had helped her lead several people to Christ. Not long after meeting Eddie, she began taking him to church where he, too, accepted the Lord. After a courtship of sixteen months, Eileen and Eddie were married at the altar.

Shortly afterward, as Eddie was finishing law school, she tried to prevail on the attorneys at her firm to make a place for him, too. When they declined, Eileen and Eddie decided to start their own firm, hoping to pool their talents in jurisprudence.

Eileen and Eddie did everything together from office work to racquetball. Eddie was content and found Eileen exciting. He had never possessed much spontaneity, and living in the same house with Eileen broadened his horizons socially as well as spiritually. They rarely argued. But when they did, Eddie drove Eileen almost to the brink. He would lie down on the couch, spread the newspaper in front of him, flick on the TV and shut her out.

At church Eileen and Eddie had a lot of friends, since Eileen had taken the trouble to cultivate relationships. Eddie had no friends of his own and relied on her. He relied on her in other areas, too. In fact, it seemed to Eileen that when it came to figuring out what needed to be done and actually doing it, Eddie was paralyzed. When he did move, it was at a snail's pace. She took over more of the decision-making.

What was important to Eddie was people's feelings. He hated confrontation and avoided conversations in which conflict might emerge. He was content in their firm to do research and other tasks requiring limited interaction. When he did interact, it was usually in *pro bono* cases for people who needed help. Eddie had a soothing touch to calm the frightened and a level head to determine the best course of action. Implementation, on the other hand, was a problem.

It was not long before Eileen and Eddie's professional friends perceived them as an aggressive female/passive male combination. At church she was viewed as not submissive to her husband. Eddie was viewed as a man "out of divine order" who let his wife lead him.

To the casual Christian observer it seemed that Eileen should step back, take a few deep breaths and let Eddie take charge. But whenever Eileen tried this at work, the office began to flounder. Procrastination was Eddie's middle name. He put off financial work until the last minute. He prepared briefs the night before he appeared in court and sometimes lost cases because of inadequate research.

Periodically they talked the problem over. Eileen would let it go until she felt the firm was suffering and she couldn't take it anymore; then she would plead tearfully with Eddie to try harder. Eddie never protested and always promised he would, but lapsed after a few days into old habits.

When phone calls came from bill collectors or clients whose needs were not being met, Eileen covered for Eddie. She told them what all he was doing, even though she knew there were long stretches during the day when he could take care of those tasks. It was as though they were running a relay, but when it came time to hand off the baton, he would drop it.

Several years passed. Eileen kept turning over the problem of Eddie's procrastination to the Lord, asking Him for wisdom and reminding herself that He had put them together and given them wonderful children. Her pastor advised her to take a few steps back and let Eddie lead. Because Eileen loved the Lord and did not want to do anything to embarrass her husband, she tried to adjust herself to Eddie's pace. Inevitably, though, they failed and returned to old patterns. Eileen came to feel that Eddie was sabotaging their financial success (which her mother was all too quick to point out). Surely the Lord expected more in a Christian business.

Gradually, as Eileen found she could not make Eddie change, she decided to work around him at the firm. People's lives, finances and futures depended on what happened to them in court. She could not fail them and let the firm fail while continuing to wait for Eddie to get his act together. So she extricated herself from every case Eddie was working on and developed her own docket of cases.

All the while, her resentment began to build. She felt frustrated and angry with Eddie and somewhat betrayed by God, who had apparently not shown her what to do. She was beginning to buckle under the pressure of the shame of seeming to lead her husband, of holding the business together and feeling that everything depended on her. She hated to nag Eddie— nagging was the one quality she hated in her mother—but the older she grew, the more she knew she sounded just like her.

If only, Eileen thought, as the wedge between them drove them further apart, *I hadn't married the first thing that came along.*

When a Woman's Dependency Needs Go Unmet

Eileen had learned independence from watching her father's passivity create emotional conflict in her mother. Her father had procrastinated, too, about everything from home repairs to bill-paying. Unlike Eddie—a loving, playful father— Eileen's dad had never played with her and her siblings. Her caretaking instincts had been developed further from having to look after her brothers and sisters. Her mother's frequent comments about men had suggested to Eileen, moreover, that men want to depend on women.

So Eileen had taken the "hero" role of the dysfunctional home, determined to make the best of her situation, escape the trap her home had become and never depend on it. She was perfectionistic in her desire to see everything done well and often set unrealistic goals—which, though they can be admirable qualities, exert undue pressure when they develop out of the wounds suffered in childhood.

Eileen was subconsciously attracted to the man who had the positive qualities her father had. But each of those qualities had their downside (as they always do). In the blossom of their relationship, Eileen and Eddie hoped to make themselves into the healthy, happy family neither had known as children.

But Eddie was a perfectionist, too, a perfectionist of a different kind and the product of his upbringing. He had longed desperately for the approval of his father, who was often too preoccupied to notice Eddie's achievements or praise him for his strengths. So Eddie became terrified of failure and subconsciously adopted the habit of avoidance whenever failure seemed even remotely possible.

Both Eileen and Eddie hoped in their own marriage not to repeat the mistakes their parents had made. But even without the destructive factor of alcoholism, they settled after fifteen years of marriage into patterns similar to those of their parents.

Were they wrong for each other from the start?

The Pain of Being Different

The natural temperament combination of Eddie and Eileen invites the critical assessment of both society and church. Traditional views of women's roles, even in the modern world, have prescribed boundaries for women that can become constricting.

Unfortunately, the quiet, passive woman seems to many the only woman who fits the traditional biblical mold of a wife. The "gentle and quiet spirit" Peter described (1 Peter 3:4) gives life to a mental image that often passes as the biblical norm.

A woman like Eileen, capable of holding her own and even excelling in areas once exclusive to men, is often considered a usurper.

In truth, Eileen is closer to the true biblical model than the passive/aggressive woman who masks her rebellion with a facade of weakness. And Eileen's and Eddie's differences, as it turns out, are more the result of God-given traits than acquired behavior. The dysfunction in their homes of origin only exaggerated the strengths and weaknesses of their own temperaments.

There is a place for all kinds of men and women in this world. A closer observation of human nature will reveal that a large part of the population of husbands and wives are like Eileen and Eddie, the "laid-back" husband and the "vivacious and aggressive" wife.

In his book *Your Temperament: Discover Its Potential*, Tim LaHaye defines temperament as the "combination of inborn characteristics that affect our behavior." Each of four basic temperaments possesses both positive and negative characteristics. The sanguine temperament is outgoing, jovial but often compulsive. The phlegmatic is laid back, deliberate but procrastinating. The melancholic is sensitive, caring but negatively analytical. The choleric is goal-oriented, decisive but driven.[1]

Every person's temperament is a blend of all four temperaments, with two predominant. In a survey of several hundred couples, LaHaye discovered that fewer than four percent were the same temperament as their spouse. The phlegmatic-melancholics were almost always attracted to the sanguine-cholerics. (Eileen is sanguine-choleric and Eddie is phlegmatic-melancholic. Their marital conflicts are common to this temperament combination.)

LaHaye goes on to comment that "most people are completely unaware of this extremely powerful influence on their behavior. Consequently, instead of cooperating with it and using it, they conflict with this inner motivation and often try to make something of themselves that they were never intended to be. This not only limits them personally, but affects their immediate family and often spoils other interpersonal relationships."[2]

Not only is temperament a consideration, but a closer study of the Bible—of both its characters and its principles—will show that not all the godly women in it were shy violets fading into the wallpaper! The prophetess Deborah by no means fits the mold we often describe as godly in the Church today. Declaring the word of God, she led Israel onto the battlefield. The armies sought her counsel and Barak, the general, implemented her direction.

Or what do we do with the woman described in Proverbs 31 whose managerial skills matched those of the best manager in the business world today? She purchased real estate and managed a staff while setting her hand to the more traditional household chores that have come to be known as "women's work." Women like Sarah, Leah, Rachel and a host of others were often tempted into manipulative tactics (as we noted earlier) because they were shut out of active decision-making in their homes.

Are the qualities Eileen exhibited the products of a sin-sick life or of sexual perversion? Ironically, the very qualities that make such a woman attractive to a man like Eddie are those that many Christians say she should not have. Should she squelch her natural talents, quench her spiritual gifts? Is her only recourse being considered forever "out of order"?

The biblical admonition to wives to "be subject to your own husbands" (Ephesians 5:22) affords great freedom in the marital relationship. As we look now at the meaning of true intimacy in marriage, you will see that submission does not mean changing your personality to fit the mold of another. Rather, submitting or fitting into your husband's life means learning how your strengths complement his weaknesses, and vice versa. If your husband has chosen you to be his mate, changing yourself to fit another man's concept of what a Christian wife "should" be is really out of divine order.

Remember, too, that Eileen is not the only half of the couple criticized for natural tendencies. Eddie and many gentle men like him are afforded less honor in a world that prizes aggression and puts a premium on machismo. Although the image of the macho male is nowhere in keeping with the fruit of the Holy Spirit, a church is often led by men who feel that it shows strength of character to get along without women except for the provision of sexual needs, procreation and "less important" chores. While they bar women from the board room and the pulpit, the very purpose for which woman was created—to help man—is jeopardized.

Eddie was genuinely glad for Eileen's success in the legal profession and praised her often, privately and publicly. But it bothered him that others cast him as weak. Eileen knew better than anyone that her husband was strong in less obvious ways—that he held firm convictions, for instance, and preserved them in spite of the influence of others.

In reality, Eileen and Eddie were as right for each other as any two could be. But responsible in part for the widening gap between them was their deep-seated emotional response to the unfair characterizations of others. When they began to recognize this, they learned to eradicate the gap between them and solve their problem. It all began with a deeper understanding of the Word of God.

A Suitable Helper

When God created man and breathed the breath of life into his nostrils, the woman was still inside of him. God watched Adam for a season and observed, "It is not good for the man to be alone; I will make him a helper suitable for him" (Genesis 2:18). It was when God determined that for man to be by himself was not good that He moved to finish His creation.

Causing a deep sleep to fall upon Adam, God opened his flesh (verse 21) and removed one of Adam's sides. The word *tsela* in Hebrew means "side" rather than "rib." In fact, the word *tsela* is not translated "rib" anywhere else in the Bible. In what may have been a formative process more akin to cell division than surgery, woman was taken out of man. She was not merely "bone of his bone," as if she were made from a rib alone, but also "flesh of his flesh" (Genesis 2:23).[3]

The relationship between man and woman knew no conflict, disagreement or sense of competitiveness. They were one, each incomplete without the other, intent on carrying out the commands of the Lord. They were blessed by God and given one assignment: "Be fruitful and multiply, and fill the earth, and subdue it; and rule over the fish of the sea and over the birds of the sky, and over every living thing that moves on the earth" (Genesis 1:28). God also made the Garden and gave one purpose within it: "To cultivate it and keep it" (2:15). The woman was created to help man carry out this purpose.

The word *helper* is the word *ezer*, found in verses like Psalm 54:4: "God is my helper." We may thus surmise that woman was not inferior help but an equal, created by the Lord. Before the Fall there was no sense of inferiority or superiority; woman was merely different, containing by nature the parts of the man used to create her. He would never again be complete without her. To look at woman was to see everything man was not. When the woman looked at Adam, she, too, saw everything she was not. They fit together to fulfill the commandments of the Lord.

It was for this reason, I believe, that the Bible says the man and his wife were naked and not ashamed. To see each other brought a sense of completion. And I doubt that they were ever alone. They needed each other, since being alone was not good in God's sight. They were together in their work and in the presence of God. God wanted to see them together when they fellowshiped with Him in the cool of the day.

The relationship man and woman had before the Fall is the picture of true unity. It was not until sin perverted creation that we read of competition between them or the exaltation of one sex over the other.

And this picture of competition changed forever once Jesus ascended into heaven and sent the Helper, the Holy Spirit. As He fills men and women, we may together once again be blessed and anointed to fulfill the purposes of God. When a married couple have an enlightened understanding of their needs and are open to the help God is sending them in the other, marital conflict subsides and each spouse is honored and respected.

Each sex, therefore, has dependency needs that must be met. The key to meeting those needs is the key to intimacy. It begins by discovering the innermost needs of each spouse and collaborating to fill those needs.

Let's return to the case of Eileen and Eddie. Instead of fitting together, Eileen and Eddie had divided emotionally into two distinct parts independent of one another. As the dependency needs of each went unmet, the gap widened.

Eddie's procrastination was exaggerating Eileen's unmet need to feel protected from shame and financial disaster. Eileen's nagging showed that she was trying to fill in the gaps she saw in him. She wound up being codependent, adapting to Eddie's weakness rather than filling it.

As Eddie's weakness magnified, he began to shut Eileen emotionally from his life. Once again, it seemed to him, he was failing. He could not be accepted for who he was and be loved unconditionally. His hurt was exaggerated by all outside expectations that he act as independent of female help as his observers pretended to be. Instead of the two spouses drawing closer, each became more independent.

Happily, Eddie and Eileen began to understand, with God's help, the nature of intimacy, and to heal the emotional breach between them.

The Key to Intimacy

It began the day Eileen broke emotionally in front of Eddie. She hated to make a scene because Eddie usually just stared at her. But this time was different.

"Please, Eddie," she blurted out one day, "it feels like we're spinning in different worlds, growing farther and farther apart. There's something about you I can't touch. I feel so ashamed."

Letting out years of fear and pain, Eileen was astonished to see tears well up in Eddie's eyes.

"It's not that I don't care," he said haltingly, choking back the tears. "I know I'm hurting you. But I'm hurting myself. Every time I know there's something I ought to do, it seems that in front of me is a large mountain I'm unable to climb. The things that seem so easy to everyone else . . . frighten me."

As Eddie tried to express his deepest private pain, Eileen began to feel compassion. He was finally trusting her with his most shameful fear.

"I'm really not trying to hurt you," he continued, amid long pauses. "But every day there's a mountain in the way. I'm ashamed I'm this way. It's like I'm handicapped. . . . "

Eileen listened, aware that a wall between them was cracking. As Eddie went on, the loneliness of being shut out of the deepest level of his life began to evaporate, along with the anger and frustration of fighting an enemy she could not see.

She sat next to Eddie, admitting the pressure she had placed on him with her perfectionism, then hugged him quietly for several minutes. In a moment of enlightenment, Eileen realized where she could most help Eddie. He was finally asking her to help him where his natural strength failed.

Eileen broke the silence. "We'll climb the mountain together. Whatever it takes, one mountain at a time, we'll do it together."

As they talked, Eileen was filled with a desire to be physically close to Eddie, to be intimate. She had never felt more loved. Her worth as the kind of woman God created her to be was finally validated at the spiritual level. They were truly one. Gone was the desire to be involved in her own pursuits to the exclusion of his. He needed her—not in a codependent but in an interdependent way.

Eileen and Eddie's sex life had been very good in spite of the difficulties, but the intimacy they had once experienced had been disrupted. Now, once Eddie had disclosed his spiritual and emotional need, Eileen knew he had given her the highest form of trust. He had "disrobed" himself emotionally and spiritually in her presence.

Intercourse became the punctuation mark to a deeper emotional intimacy than they had known previously. Their desire for one another was marked by a sense of closeness in the spiritual dimension. Eileen and Eddie found that they were indeed one flesh. God had used the conflict they had been experiencing for their good.

Such is the redemptive power of Jesus Christ in operation in the most intimate human relationship. In the light of this understanding, it is easier to understand why lust and its extensions—sexual abuse, infidelity, homosexuality, pornography, premarital sex and masturbation—are all perversions of the highest form of human intimacy, the spiritual union that takes place when man and woman join physically in intercourse. The perversions are all ways of saying, "I can do without you." This is why they defile the marriage bed and heighten shame rather than remove it. Substituting them for the pure form of intimacy between husband and wife suggests the presence of the fear of self-disclosure.

Communication difficulties inhibit the highest form of sexual intimacy, which comes only when one is completely open and vulnerable to the other. When a couple is preoccupied or having difficulty communicating, emotional or physical satisfaction is inevitably lacking.

The Endearing Power of Self-Disclosure

Experiencing genuine intimacy is the key to removing loneliness. And the secret of intimacy in all relationships, not just in marriage, is learning the art of self-disclosure. One result of the Fall in human beings is a deep sense of abandonment, a longing to be touched by others who will disclose themselves, their failures and weaknesses as well as their strengths.

Shame also came about at the Fall, and shame prevents self-disclosure. When human beings feel ashamed or fearful, we move away from intimacy. This principle can be observed in every human relationship—husband-wife, parent-child, friend-friend and professional relationships as well as relationships between members of the Body of Christ. It can even be observed in the relationship between a public speaker and his audience. The one who speaks without shame over who he is causes the audience to feel close to him and enjoy listening to him. The speaker who hides behind a mask robs himself and others of that sense of closeness.

Although marriage is the most intimate human relationship, the single adult is in no way consigned to a life of loneliness. The single woman able to disclose herself emotionally and spiritually will find many friends. People are hungry for intimacy on levels other than marital intimacy, and the tendency to group individuals on the basis of age and marital status often robs us of healthy interaction.

One of my closest friends in our congregation is a single woman. Pam, an art teacher at the Falk School and the University of Pittsburgh, has been a member of our congregation for nearly fifteen years and has matured socially, spiritually and emotionally faster than many people ever do. She may not know that her own secret is the ability to disclose her innermost thoughts and feelings to those she trusts.

But Pam is no emotional exhibitionist, a flaw in many people afflicted with codependency. Longing for friends, they disclose inappropriate details of their personal lives in order to draw attention from others. People who talk compulsively or complain about their problems are really masking their true needs and using external conflicts as "fig leaves" to prevent self-disclosure on a deeper level. Those who use their friends as counselors all the time drain the relationship rather than give to it.

Pam's friends could not wait to throw a surprise party for her this year. Married couples as well as singles jumped at the chance to honor her. She is a pleasure to be near.

Self-disclosure endears a woman not only to husband and friends, but to God. When we disclose ourselves to Him, we admit our need for His fellowship as well as His power. Exposing your deepest thoughts and feelings to God is always rewarded by His self-disclosure.

Jesus revealed the criteria for God's self-disclosure: "He who has My commandments and keeps them, he it is who loves Me; and he who loves Me shall be loved by My Father, and I will love him, and will disclose Myself to him" (John 14:21). Disclosing ourselves brings us to a place of intimacy with God. Someone has said, "A friend is someone who knows all about you and loves you just the same." Whether it is friendship with God, with one's spouse or with others, learning the art of self-disclosure is the key to all intimate friendships.

Eileen and Eddie: Beyond Crisis

The initial phase of any relationship usually involves fantasized notions that obscure reality. This creates the hope phase in the hope/disappointment roller coaster. Crises usually shatter the fantasy; then disillusionment sets in. Once the negatives are seen, each party in the relationship must be willing to accept them. They must also be committed to continued self-disclosure, or else the relationship—whether between spouses, friends, pastor and congregation, or boss and employee—will reach an impasse, stagnate, even die.

Men and women who come from dysfunctional homes are more prone to fantasizing away negatives in the hope phase of their new relationships, only to discover that their unrealistic expectations are not and often cannot be met. The new relationship is often discarded before it has a chance to develop. A healthy relationship is impossible until the crisis is reached, the fantasy-created bubble of denial is broken and the relationship has passed through the valley of disappointment. Discovering which expectations are realistic and whether the other party can meet them are the principal factors in the development of healthy long-term relationships.

Once Eileen and Eddie passed the crisis in their relationship, their marriage bond began to strengthen. They decided to commit themselves to one another's weaknesses, which they had either not discovered or not understood thoroughly before their marriage vows.

Seeing potential problems before marriage is far different from experiencing their emotional impact later. Many people underestimate this emotional impact and either commit themselves too quickly to marriage or else quit the marriage when crisis brings disappointment and forces them to face the negatives. If Eileen and Eddie had not committed themselves to one another's weaknesses, they would have gone the way of many Christian couples who believe that divorce is not an option: living under the same roof but continuing on separate paths, far from the joy of real marriage.

After several halting efforts, Eileen and Eddie developed signals to let the other know when help was needed. They took practical steps, such as brief meetings during the day and facing awkward confrontations together. They are still married and practicing law together. As they have accepted and validated one another, they are discovering they are more in love than ever.

The women in the next chapter, by contrast, have allowed their unhealed emotional wounds to fester into a contempt for men. Let's examine the origin and results of man-hatred.

8

. . . .

The Woman Who Hates Men

Answer yes or no to the following questions:

_____ 1. Have you ever been deeply hurt by a man?

_____ 2. Did your own father validate your appearance, your feelings and your accomplishments with love and affirmation for who you were, not just what you could do?

_____ 3. Were you ever violated sexually?

_____ 4. Do you "freeze" emotionally when you are alone with a man?

_____ 5. Do you often feel angry over the injustices women undergo in our society?

_____ 6. Do you secretly feel that most men are out for what they can get from a woman?

_____ 7. Did your father abuse you verbally, call you names or accuse you?

_____ 8. Did your mother have a negative or demeaning attitude toward men?

_____ 9. Did your father treat your mother with respect?

_____ 10. Do you have a strong need for male approval?

_____ 11. Do you secretly enjoy flirting with men?

_____ 12. Do you like to be in places where you have power over men?

_____ 13. Do you attract a man and, when he wants to further the relationship, drop him?

_____ 14. Do you become jealous and possessive in female relationships, wanting the exclusive rights of friendship with another woman?

_____ 15. Have you ever been attracted sexually to another woman?

_____ 16. Have you developed negative generalizations about men?

Yes answers to all questions except #2 and #9, and no answers to those two, indicate that you are set up to develop a negative attitude toward men. You may be moving from an honest concern over the plight of women to a contempt for men.

When a woman's dependency needs remain unmet in her primary relationships with males, her natural instinct of self-preservation makes her determined to live without them. And while it is healthy for a single woman to be independent in life while dependent on the Lord, it is unhealthy to despise the interdependence between men and women.

Leigh had a childhood that was the perfect setup for this attitude.

Getting Back at Men

As early as Leigh can remember, her father made it clear that he wanted her, the youngest of three daughters, to be a boy, a son to carry on his name. Leigh grew up searching desperately for his approval, which she got only when she excelled athletically. She played softball (as close to Little League as a girl could get at the time), which made her dad happy. But before long she was characterized as a tomboy or tough girl. She grew to despise feminine things and refused as she got older to wear dresses, makeup and jewelry. She projected a masculine air and intimidated other girls, for whom she had little use.

Then in high school Leigh's attention became riveted on Tom, a member of the football team. By this time she had played the boyish role so long that the boys looked at her as one of the gang. Tom never looked her way at all. It was difficult and embarrassing for Leigh to break the mold, to step outside the character she played. To do so, she felt, would bring on the ridicule of the girls. Not until after graduation did she make her first halting steps toward femininity.

Leigh and her mother had never been close. Her mother had not known how to communicate with her boyish daughter and had felt rejected when Leigh spent her life trying to please her father. When he died, she was left with a daughter she barely knew. Attempts at conversation were awkward and Leigh's basketball scholarship to college was a welcome relief.

But college for Leigh proved to be little happier than high school. It was not long before Sean in her Spanish class began to show an interest in her. One thing led to another and by the time the first semester was over Leigh had fallen for him. He showed her the first male affirmation of her womanhood and she went to bed with him frequently. But Sean's true feelings for Leigh were no more than a passing interest. By her sophomore year Sean was seeing other women. Leigh felt betrayed and her anger at Sean turned to hatred.

It was then that Reed came in to pick up the pieces and restore hope. Leigh fell for Reed within a few days, fantasizing that he was the knight who would save her self-esteem. Her relationship with Reed peaked fast. On the second date they slept together and within three weeks Reed seemed to be losing interest. No phone calls, avoidance in class.

In an effort to rescue her bruised emotions, Leigh hit the books and was seldom seen outside the library. Determined to hide from further hurt, she resolved to prove she could make it in a man's world. Subconsciously she made the decision to get even. Her appearance reverted to the boyish style she had adopted in high school and she toughened her emotions, too.

By the time Leigh was thirty she was a stockbroker. Her highly competitive nature caused her to excel. She was a risk-taker usually rewarded with success. Despite a vicious streak that lost her clients and kept other brokers out of her way, her chutzpah was just what management wanted and won her promotions. Leigh secretly relished her triumph over the men around her as though she had conquered at last.

Meanwhile, Leigh's cousin had been talking to her about the Lord. One day she happened into a church thinking to assuage her conscience over an unethical business deal. The visiting evangelist's message was powerful and Leigh was swept into the Kingdom.

Leigh's Christian life was not easy. She harbored pangs of conscience when her business decisions conflicted with Christian values, but she feared financial failure, which would mean vulnerability in a world where financial freedom was her last bastion of security. Surely God understood, she thought. Leigh became expert at overriding her conscience.

At church she quickly gained the attention of the pastor and his wife and other leaders who valued her business sense and obvious capability. She was put in charge of projects but could not stand the weak-willed men and women around her—except for Patricia, a single mother who responded to Leigh's strength in the wake of a messy divorce.

Leigh, in her loneliness, was drawn to Patricia's need. She visited Patricia constantly and began to be jealous when others "intruded" on their relationship. Leigh spent money on Patricia, giving her appliances and furniture, gifts on her birthday and holidays and even paying her attorney's fees. But there were strings attached. Leigh wanted Patricia's exclusive attention to ease the isolation she felt from men. Anyone who posed a threat was dispatched with subtle forms of manipulation until Patricia was exclusively Leigh's property.

Although people at church thought they were inseparable friends, they did not know that both Leigh's and Patricia's unhealed emotional wounds were propelling them on a dark course toward perversion. Leigh and Patricia looked to each other for the affection and affirmation they did not receive from men, and became sexual partners, keeping that secret from those in church who "wouldn't understand." Leigh felt no remorse; her conscience had already been divorced from her spirit.

If Patricia had not broken down emotionally, they might still be involved today, in a life devoid of any need for men.

The Path toward Perversion

Patricia awakened one day realizing that she had become a lesbian. She had often wondered how such a thing happened between women, something she had always found deeply revolting. Unlike Leigh, Patricia was sensitive to guilt, having been brought up under a Christian influence. Still, her past contained many poison ingredients: rejection by her father, an overprotective mother, disappointments with men and a passive will that gave in to domination in the wake of emotional disaster.

Leigh's "advances" had been disguised as generosity and concern for her welfare. Because Patricia could not bear the loss of the security and friendship she found in Leigh, she had failed to observe the warning signs in Leigh's possessiveness and violent temper, which she feared. Patricia was an easy target for control and Leigh, like a lion isolating its prey, found Patricia's vulnerability enticing.

Leigh was stronger spiritually, it seemed to Patricia, and she looked to her for advice about everything. Leigh put down men, categorizing them as enemies intent on her demise. Gradually Patricia's own mistrust of men grew until she was isolated even from her pastor, whom she had always admired.

Rationalizing away shame is easy when you are angry, and Leigh's and Patricia's anger toward men gradually tore away the last barrier to sin. Why not? Surely God understood that sexual needs do not just go away. Gratification with another woman was justified and safe. Perhaps she was born this way. Her thoughts began to be invaded with seemingly logical answers to all her arguments against physical involvement and served to shore up her weakening conscience. This, coupled with her need for approval, locked her into Leigh's controlling influence.

Demonic influences prey upon an individual's emotional wounds, custom-fitting into any situation and leading him wherever they want him to go. Patricia had been victimized in her emotional wounds without realizing it and seduced into compliance.

What happened to Patricia is a classic lesson in seduction, the misleading power that overcomes a weakened individual and causes him or her to violate conscience and reason in the interest of self-gratification. Seduction happens all the time in one form or another over what might be considered less serious sins. Very often deception is occurring simultaneously, preventing the victim from knowing that seduction is taking place. Before long it is too late and his will is too weak to resist further invasion. The end of seduction is sin against God, others and oneself. Its momentum is fed by guilt until one day the conscience no longer reacts to sin at all.

Feminism and the Church

What is Patricia and Leigh's story doing in a Christian book about restoring wounded women? Because of the marked increase in lesbian and homosexual activity in evangelical and charismatic circles. Pastors and Christian leaders are sharing with me that it is increasingly common to encounter women who have been seduced into this lifestyle. What was once considered unthinkable has now become tolerated and even accepted. Handling the situation in a redemptive way, once it is discovered, and healing the parties involved proves difficult.

The anger and resentment women feel toward victimization by men can polarize them against men in general, setting women up for sexual and other forms of seduction. Sometimes their anger against or fear of men is so deep that it is unrecognized and unacknowledged; yet its undisclosed presence affects them all the same. And often it leads them to embrace the causes of a more radical sector of society.

The Christian woman cannot afford to unconditionally embrace radical feminism, which has developed as a backlash against an evil in society—the discrimination against women. It is true that the radical element of a society can tilt social ills that are off balance back into balance. A radical voice can, by overcompensating, exert enough pressure to pull society back toward fairness.

But this does not mean extremism is the answer. The Christian woman has no call to wrestle against flesh and blood. Although my own views intersect with feminism on several issues, and while I applaud many changes in society that have come as a result of the new awareness of the plight of women, I oppose the idea that most men are misogynists and that one sex should be exalted above the other. Radical feminists can, like any movement, quickly become motivated by anger and hatred, which will ultimately not achieve the righteousness of God.

God has called the Christian woman, rather, to a position of rest in our war with evil. Our job is to occupy, posturing ourselves firmly but non-aggressively on the boundaries Jesus Christ has already won for us. It is Jesus who is working for woman, opening the way for her wherever He wants her to be. My own path into the position of woman minister and co-pastor of our church was not cleared by the feminist movement but by Jesus Christ when He defeated my enemy at Calvary. It is He who gives me any right or ability to take such a role. Because of Him, I do not have to adopt the hatred of men as my posture or use any other carnal weapon to achieve victory for myself or for other women. Jesus Christ, not the feminist movement, is our liberator.

Nor is the Church being victimized, in my opinion, by the radical feminist element of society. Rather, the Church is undergoing a change instituted by the Holy Spirit to remove the prejudice within her that has bound women for centuries.

The devil is working hard to counter this work of the Holy Spirit. He is working, on the one hand, to boost the extremism that leads to the hatred of men. And he is working, on the other hand, to deceive earnest Christians into believing that any emphasis on women's rights is satanic.

I mentioned before that Christian women cannot afford to embrace radical feminism. But neither can we ignore the advancement of women. We cannot look at the agenda of the feminist movement, such as man-hatred, lesbianism and abortion, and turn in fear from needed changes. This is Satan's trick to turn the Church on herself. Our weapon against this deception is not a carnal one, but rather the revelation of Jesus Christ in the Word of God.

The Holy Spirit is moving in the Church today to raise women up (as we will discuss in another chapter) to release

His power in them, ultimately to exalt Jesus Christ. Our victory as the Body of Christ will be achieved when all hindrances to the exaltation of the name of Jesus are removed.

Jezebels at Work

Paul wrote Timothy that in the last times many people would wander from the faith, victims of seducing spirits. Whether or not we are living in the last days is debatable, depending on what church you go to, but one thing is sure: Today we are closer to the end than we were yesterday. And whether we die now or live until the end times, we are all closer to our own "last days."

In the book of Revelation, John warned the church at Thyatira, "You tolerate the woman Jezebel, who calls herself a prophetess, and she teaches and leads My bond-servants astray, so that they commit acts of immorality and eat things sacrificed to idols" (Revelation 2:20). Perhaps this was a real woman who tormented the church at Thyatira, or perhaps it was a figurative name for a deluding influence resembling the controlling queen of Israel who hated Elijah. Either way, people like Jezebel, men and women, are found everywhere there is unacknowledged anger against one sex or another, wounds that are unhealed and an overwhelming need to control.

The Jezebel of the Old Testament grew up the child of the king of the Sidonians. She grew up learning to fear Baal and witnessing the acts of child sacrifice and sexual perversion that accompanied the worship of this heathen god. Who knows (since the household devoted to Baal knew no moral bounds) what dysfunction troubled her home? Jezebel may have grown up sexually abused and wondering if she, too, would wind up on the smoldering altar. Emotional abuse undoubtedly toughened this woman into a force so evil that one of the greatest prophets of the Old Testament had to be raised up against her.

The Scripture curtain opens on Jezebel as the bride of King Ahab, whose spineless character became the target for her wiles and manipulation. When Ahab pouted, Jezebel acted to murder the owner of the vineyard her husband wanted. She rolled over weak-willed Ahab and set up altars to Baal throughout Israel. She systematically murdered the priest and prophets of God. And when Elijah was vindicated by the Lord on Mount Carmel and killed the prophets of Baal with the full approval of the people, Jezebel's heart was so hardened that she went after Elijah with increased vengeance. Of her influence we read in 1 Kings, "Surely there was no one like Ahab who sold himself to do evil in the sight of the Lord, because Jezebel his wife incited him" (21:25). Jezebel had the power to make her husband do anything—jeopardize his own relationship with God by idolatry, and even commit murder.

How did she do it? How did Leigh deceive Patricia? By following the three steps to deception.

Three Steps to Deception

The first step in this process is *wearing down the conscience*.

Like the Jezebel in the book of Revelation, who caused God's people to violate their consciences and eat meat offered to idols, the teacher who resembles Jezebel today causes the believer to ignore his conscience. The conscience will, if ignored, cease to respond to greater forms of evil, until the worst acts can be committed without the faintest pang.

That is how the Pharisees killed Jesus. They had so rationalized away their consciences with sanctimonious piety that they could murder an innocent man.

The second step to deception is *instilling a foundation for immoral behavior*.

In the story of Leigh and Patricia, Leigh seemed more spiritual to Patricia because she was strong. Leigh knew enough of the Scriptures to be dangerous and was quick to criticize others in the name of discernment. She intimidated Patricia with spiritual abuse. Patricia was so unsure of herself that she did not notice.

The third step is *isolation*.

Like Jezebel, Leigh seduced or led astray the vulnerable, severing any relationships that posed a threat to her exclusive control of Patricia. The feelings of isolation Patricia carried with her—the result of her unwanted divorce—lessened her means of protection, leaving her vulnerable emotionally and financially to a stronger-willed person. Once alienated from her husband, Patricia was then severed, with the help of Leigh and the enemy, from fellowship with God.

Isolation from fellowship with God and from the main-stream of the Body of Christ is always a prelude to deception, the invasion of an evil, controlling influence in a believer's life. The cults isolate their prey, and many well-meaning Christians, disillusioned with the conflict that occurs within churches, often leave and never return, opening themselves to lukewarmness.

Other sensitive Christians seeking a deep experience with the Lord experience isolation as the enemy deceives them with forms of spiritual pride that set them apart. Some believe that the Lord is drawing them aside for special revelation. During such times of isolation, Satan makes sure that a "head" other than Jesus Christ is interposed between the believer and God.

Invariably, a strong-willed person like Leigh will separate her subject from the influence of other spiritual persons in her life, such as the pastor and leaders of her church. If Leigh's opinion differed from that of the pastor, Patricia believed Leigh. To disagree with her was, in Leigh's eyes, to betray her. Isolation is the enemy of restoration. And since abiding in Christ is the secret of fruitfulness, severing Patricia from the Holy Spirit's influence in her life provided the opportunity for seduction and deception.

Acts of immorality followed as a matter of course. Leigh seduced Patricia systematically into submitting. This is not to say Patricia was without guilt in this situation. Patricia did not want to admit what was happening, she did not resist it and embedded herself in a cocoon of denial. But remaining hopelessly entangled with Leigh was not the life Patricia wanted. When she finally woke up to see what she had allowed to happen to herself, she was overwhelmed with guilt. If she did not act quickly, she knew she would be too weak to fight and would succumb permanently.

Getting Healed

When Patricia broke down and told her pastor her horrible secret, it was the most shameful experience of her life. Her pastor knew, fortunately, that while he could help her spiritually, he needed the help of trained professional Christian counselors to help her regain her emotional health. Such a perception on his part displayed spiritual maturity and godly wisdom. It also showed his own emotional health.

He discerned immediately that Leigh had been victimized by a seductive spiritual influence, which was demonic. He took the necessary steps to help Patricia flee this influence, but he did not know what had made her vulnerable emotionally to spiritual attack. What may take a pastor years to discern may take a well-trained professional counselor only a few minutes. (Bill and I have discovered the wealth of help the Lord has provided in our area in Christian counselors with sound biblical foundations.)

While the pastor's focus on the spiritual life is vital, I believe the Lord is awakening the Church to the fact that emotional wounds can quench the Holy Spirit and render some forms of spiritual help only temporary. When a person suffers emotional damage, he or she is less able to hold onto spiritual revelation. Thus, as Jesus taught, the demons go out into the dry places seeking rest and, finding none, they return to their original house, swept clean now but still open for business (see Matthew 12:43-45).

The prophet Jeremiah prophesied for the Lord: "I will restore you to health and I will heal you of your wounds" (Jeremiah 30:17). Jesus characterized Himself as the Good Shepherd, the restorer of souls, and announced at the beginning of His ministry that He was here (among other things) to heal the brokenhearted. Whenever a person's broken heart and emotional wounds are healed, the person can grasp and retain spiritual truth. Until that healing occurs, the pastor can pour into a person continually and find the wineskin continually leaking. The problem is not the delivery of the message but the container itself.

Patricia's pastor was confident in the ministry of the professional Christian counselors to whom he referred Patricia. He knew that they would support his own ministry as well as bring Patricia to the next step in the healing process. (Note: In the case of lesbianism and homosexuality, only Christian psychiatrists and psychologists are likely to be of aid, since these aberrations have been removed from the *Diagnostic and Statistical Manual III of Psychological Disorders* subscribed to by secular counselors.)

Breaking Ties

Treatment for Patricia began with severing all ties with Leigh. Patricia did not know how attached she had become until this moment. It was like going through another divorce, this time without the sympathy of her friends. Patricia wisely let her pastor confront Leigh. He asked Leigh to attend another church, suggesting she counsel with the pastor there and a Christian psychiatrist. This helped Patricia begin to distance herself from Leigh and it gave Leigh the opportunity to heal, too.

Patricia was advised by her counselors to reenter the straight world and begin by attending various services at church. Forbidden were places and activities she and Leigh had done together, as Patricia was to distance herself from sentimental reminders of the past.

Fleeing the Jezebel-like influence is necessary for someone in an emotionally or spiritually weakened condition or when there is no hope of resolving the conflicts associated with it. King David had to get out of Saul's palace. Elijah had to escape from Jezebel after the victory on Mount Carmel. Jesus' parents fled with Him from Herod into Egypt. Jesus evaded the traps the Pharisees set for Him by disappearing into the crowd. Paul fled from people out to kill him and encouraged Timothy to flee youthful lusts.

The controlling powers of people with this manipulative ability can often destroy spiritual lives and reputations. Separating from their influence is crucial to healing. And humbly recognizing our own weakness in the face of it is the first step to victory. But the devil loves to use a victim's pride to seduce him or her into open conflict, further damaging the Body of Christ.

Only when Leigh's controlling influence was removed could Patricia's therapists open her emotional wounds to the light of God's grace. One by one her relationships with men were opened and her pain validated. It took almost two years, but she finally moved through each one to the place where she could forgive not just with her head, but with her heart—her ex-husband, father, mother and, finally, Leigh. But just as an alcoholic must never have another drink, so Patricia cannot afford even one conversation with Leigh.

Leigh did not stay in therapy or even in church. She grew to resent her pastor, a male authority figure, and finally left. Carrying with her the emotional baggage of her past has all but smothered her spiritual life. She has grown hardened toward God and embittered toward the church that she feels "exposed" her. Those who know her wonder if she ever had a real new birth experience. Only Leigh knows. But until she submits to the restoration process, she will undoubtedly victimize others with her controlling powers and her root of bitterness.

Patricia continues to heal, a testimony to the grace of God who loves the sinner, regardless of shame, and stands ready to restore. It may be years before Patricia feels free to enter any more close friendships with men or women, but she feels comfortable in groups of Christian friends. And she takes comfort in the words of Paul concerning homosexuals: "Such were some of you; but you were washed, but you were sanctified, but you were justified in the name of the Lord Jesus Christ, and in the Spirit of our God" (1 Corinthians 6:11).

Fear, the Root of Sin

What happened when Leigh seduced Patricia represents the perversion of a woman's power to influence. The power to seduce is not limited to women, of course. Men may also possess the power of seduction to sin and dominate another man or woman's life. Nor is homosexuality the only manifestation of seduction. Misogynism is another extreme form, as is any form of abuse in which the controller comes between his victim and God.

Controllers like Leigh (and other abusers) dominate out of the fear of abandonment. Saul, Israel's king who lost his office due to disobedience to God, was overwhelmed by fear and insecurity, driven to control and manipulate everyone around him. While man is sinful by nature, the precipitating cause of sin is usually some form of fear. Almost every sin is rooted in the fear that some tangible form of security will be lost, resulting in abandonment. Even the love of money is rooted in the fear that there will not be enough.

The fear of abandonment is the root of sin in people like Leigh whose emotional wounds early in life leave them longing for affirmation and affection. Leigh's disappointments with her father and her college boyfriends caused her to displace her anger onto men in general. She became afraid of what they could do to her and vowed that she would never be vulnerable to them again. Her business dealings reflected her resolve to trample male victims in a subconscious effort to even the score.

Leigh's fear of men caused her to become dysfunctional in her ability to love. But the power of the Gospel is shown in the fact that God's perfect love casts out fear. When a wounded woman opens herself to the love of God through others, and others are able to give it, restoration always takes place.

So far we have witnessed the seductive power of Satan slithering into the lives of others to wound and destroy a woman. Now let's look at the destructive effect a woman's own unhealed wounds can have on her life and that of her family.

9

• •

A Woman's Wounds: Setup to Destruction

Supply honest answers to the following questions:

_____ 1. Do I tend to fall for men who are not good for me?

_____ 2. Have I ever been sexually violated by a man against my will?

_____ 3. Have I given away sex as a means of holding a man's interest?

_____ 4. Do I find that I will do all the giving in a relationship?

_____ 5. Do I need the approval of others to feel good about myself?

_____ 6. Was I verbally, sexually, physically or emotionally abused as a child, as a teenager or now?

_____ 7. Do I know I should break the relationship but seem unable to do it?

_____ 8. If I break up with a man who is not good for me, do I feel guilty for doing so or feel sorry for him?

_____ 9. Am I desperately afraid of being lonely?

_____ 10. Do I subconsciously look for affirmation from men?

_____ 11. Do I like my looks and personality?

_____ 12. Am I afraid that if I let go of this relationship I will never have another?

_____ 13. No matter how he treats me, do I go running back for more?

_____ 14. Was my mother abused by my father?

_____ 15. Do I jump from one absorbing interest to another?

_____ 16. Do I tend to read the first few chapters of several books rather than read one book through before starting the next?

_____ 17. Is there a trail of broken relationships behind me?

_____ 18. Do I need excitement or stimulation in my life in order to be fulfilled?

_____ 19. Did my father fail to affirm my femininity or fill my need for male approval?

_____ 20. Have I been taken advantage of time and again by those whose affection I want?

_____ 21. Have I ever had an affair with another man even though I am married to a man who is kind?

_____ 22. Do I fantasize from time to time about sexual involvement with another man?

Yes answers indicate that you are suffering from the symptoms of compulsive behavior that are manifesting in relationship addiction.

Shelley's Secret

Shelley called me from a phone booth to make a counseling appointment and attempted to hide with a self-confident manner the deep insecurity that surfaced during our brief conversation. Her meeting with me had to be kept secret because she was the wife of an elder at a church in another city where I had taught at a women's retreat. When she arrived for the appointment, it was clear she was testing me.

"I've been a Christian for thirteen years," she quipped, "and I've never heard anyone teach that we're to give anyone a break!" As she unfolded her story, I knew it would take the grace of God to give her the "break" she needed.

Shelley was involved in a clandestine affair, committing adultery against her faithful husband of fifteen years. Hoping no one would find out, least of all her pastor and Christian friends, Shelley sought a safe atmosphere to pour out her story.

She was a talented member of her church choir. After months of hard work for their Easter cantata, she had felt let down and sluggish. Then another woman in the church suggested she become part of the semi-professional choir downtown. She agreed, believing that the polish it would give her would improve her church's music ministry.

That is where the trouble began. For the first time in years, Shelley was thrown in with a new group of people unlike her friends at church. These were professional people whose interests stimulated her intellectually and creatively—something her soul had been starved for ever since her conversion experience when she gave up "fleshly" pursuits for the Lord. Having thought her behavior somewhat extreme, her husband, Bert, was glad to see Shelley happy again and encouraged her to do all she could to develop her talents.

Shelley flung herself into the choir as she did into everything she did. For the first concert, she was selected to take the alto part of a quartet. Also chosen was Lou, a local college professor whose unhappy marriage was a frequent topic of his conversation. Shelley could not imagine what Lou's wife failed to see in him. He was charming and handsome, and conversations with him were absorbing. Perhaps, she thought, she could win him to the Lord.

Several times before the first concert, Shelley stayed after practice to talk to Lou, once late into the evening. At first they were accompanied by other members of the choir, but the others would leave one by one until Lou and Shelley were alone. Their talks became more intimate.

After that first concert, Shelley felt the same letdown she had felt after the Easter cantata at church. And now she found she could not stop thinking about Lou. She missed their conversations and the way he made her feel. She was glad when only three weeks later rehearsals started again. She was chosen to work with Lou on another piece, this time a duet.

By the time of the next concert, their relationship had deepened. The self-disclosure of their late-night conversations had bred intimacy between them. And although Shelley loved her husband, Lou had opened up new horizons for her. They began kissing passionately in his car in the dark parking lot after rehearsals; then he invited her to a motel. Several times she declined, but her inhibitions were weakening as guilt overtook her. Before long she agreed to go.

Sitting in church on Sunday morning with her children after having been involved physically with Lou only the night before was difficult. It was hard to reconcile the two experiences as well as continue to conceal her feelings from Bert. Realizing she was in too deep, Shelley was now coming to me for help.

But it became evident that her idea of help meant handling a lifetime of compulsive behavior in one session. Her approach to living had always been intense involvement without long-term commitment. As she quickly unfolded her life's story, it was easy to see how she had fallen into the trap of adultery.

Her father was an alcoholic and her mother denied his alcoholism until his dying day. Missing was his affirmation in Shelley's life. Never once had he expressed acceptance of her for herself. He rarely praised her for anything except her accomplishments. Shelley was so hungry for male approval that by high school she was completely boy-crazy. On her first date she went to a country Western dance, wound up drunk and involved in sex in the back seat of the boy's car. It became known that Shelley would give herself away, and soon she was an easy mark for many of the boys in her school.

Shelley married Bert after two years of junior college. Two years later they accepted Jesus Christ together at a Christian concert and became caught up in church activities with the same compulsive alacrity Shelley gave everything. In four years Bert became an elder at their church. When conflict erupted they moved to another church. Within a short time Shelley was involved in the choir and Bert was on the board of elders. Shelley was caught up for three more years in Bible studies, women's meetings, church services and activities at the Christian school.

Bert and Shelley loved each other and enjoyed a satisfying emotional and physical relationship. That is why Shelley could not figure out why she had allowed herself to fall so far. Determining to help herself out of this dilemma, she had gone on a personal retreat with her Bible and several Christian books hoping to find relief in their pages. But she could not get Lou off her mind. The attraction was so strong that she could think of little else but the next time they would meet.

What could she do now? Lou wanted more but Shelley knew that Bert was beginning to suspect that her interest in the choir, since she was arriving home after midnight after each rehearsal, was more than musical.

Here is why.

The Compulsive Christian Woman

The compulsive-addictive personality begins to develop in childhood. Perhaps it is the combination of temperament and environmental factors that causes the compulsive personality to seek fulfillment in external stimuli. Whether it is the high of the shopping spree or the buzz of chemical addiction, the compulsive adult lives from peak to peak and develops few (if any) coping skills for living in the valley. Unless stimulated externally, this person feels overwhelmed by a deep void.

Compulsive Christians are no different, usually substituting spiritual highs for those obtained through worldly pursuits. This often masks the fact that the root of compulsivity has never been identified and healed.

When a person becomes a Christian, the Holy Spirit comes to live inside the soul and body that had been bound for self-destruction through fleshly desires. But sometimes that person, in an attempt to let the Lord have His way, goes too far, cutting off all but spiritual activities. The soul becomes starved for stimulation, which, combined with the already compulsive personality, makes for sure entanglement with trouble.

Regardless of their standing with Christ, then, compulsive women usually have several factors in common in their backgrounds: sexual violation, low self-esteem, hunger to find acceptance from men and, at the same time (if possible), a need to control them.

The significant others in the compulsive woman's dysfunctional home of origin are often preoccupied with careers or life-controlling problems—problems that prevent their giving her emotional support. At other times she rejects the emotional support available in her home. In either case, the focus of living for the compulsive becomes filling the aching void with external stimuli, as the search for fulfillment continues throughout life.

Disappointment is likely to await the compulsive woman at every turn, especially in relationships. No person alive can fill the void for her permanently. So she moves from one relationship to another as though searching for the perfect answer to her emotional needs. Behind her is a trail of broken hearts or failed friendships, people she dropped when boredom set in or who failed to fill her need.

Seeking to define her personality in the desires of others, the compulsive woman often does not know herself. Overly anxious for the approval of others, she adjusts herself constantly to their expectations, surviving periods when she must put her own desires aside to win the much-sought acceptance. A man like Lou waiting in the wings to provide acceptance is difficult if not impossible to resist.

The compulsive woman, whose sexual barriers were invaded early in life, finds that sexual involvement provides a good high. She surrenders to any man who promises a thrill in exchange for the gratification of his own needs. Rather than seeing sex as the purest form of intimacy, the compulsive woman sees it as a means to an end—the thrill of conquest or a vehicle to take her where she wants to go.

For a compulsive-addictive woman, living out life in a monogamous relationship is difficult. Her vivid fantasy life causes her eye and heart to rove, and her past is often littered with the debris of divorce.

Whenever Shelley felt bored or otherwise unfulfilled, she began to move through the other phases of the addictive cycle—contemplation, obsession, indulgence. Back at church after going to the motel with Lou, she entered the next phase of the cycle, remorse. But she mistook remorse for true repentance, when it was really a feeble counterfeit resulting in only temporary resolve. And Shelley's addiction, like every other, gained its power from secrecy. So long as it went unchallenged, she could have Lou as well as her family.

Shelley's idea of healing was also compulsive. She was convinced that one prayer would do it all; one session of counseling would be enough to give her what she needed.

But helping Shelley to freedom in one session was impossible. She was in denial over the nature and extent of her problem. She saw it as a one-shot sin rather than an all-encompassing compulsive approach to life, and she wanted from me what she wanted from everyone—a quick-fix sliding board out of trouble, an instant answer that would allow her to stay involved in the choir and keep Lou somewhat at a distance while she learned to keep her appetite at bay.

Shelley's help would never come that way. Nothing short of a complete break with the choir would restore any hope to her marriage. Cutting off ties with Lou was essential.

But a woman like Shelley is as much addicted to men like Lou as any addict is to his substance. Regardless of how she might feel later, regardless of the consequences to her marriage, her home and her friends, Shelley was propelled by the force of a temptation more powerful than herself.

So it was no surprise to me that six months after my only session with Shelley, her husband called, looking frantically for help for his failing marriage. In spite of my exhortations to Shelley to flee the tempting situation, she had held fast. She was addicted to the kind of relationship her Christian husband could not provide. Bert had become dull to her. Nor did Shelley mind that Lou was doing little more than use her, as the boys in high school had done. She was controlled by what seemed to be a gravitational pull toward sin.

When Bert confronted her after almost a year of patience about her questionable practices, Shelley, now hardened to the Lord, tried to blame Bert for the failing bond between them. Bert asked if she would give up the choir and her newfound friends in the interest of saving their marriage, but Shelley twisted his attempts to make it seem he was restricting her boundaries and quenching her talents. Couldn't he trust her?

Deep down Shelley knew she could not even trust herself, because her barriers had long since been worn down by behavior she knew was wrong. Coming back would be too hard now. She had gone too far.

Had she thought through her course of action beforehand? Was it worth giving up a fine husband and breaking the hearts of her children? Did she know it would destroy her? Shelley had not seen the depth of her need for help. Her feeble attempts to rectify her mistake lacked a necessary element, one that would have made the difference between bondage and freedom: true self-awareness.

The Need for Self-Awareness

Every revelation of God to a human being brings that person an awareness of himself or herself. When the light of God shines, it overpowers the darkness and reveals what could not before be seen. The apostle Paul wrote in 1 Corinthians 13 that when we see the Lord, we will know Him exactly as we have been known. We will be like Him, for we will see Him as He is. And the more we know and love the Lord, the more we will find real spiritual maturity. We will be less afraid of Him because we have opened the worst sides of ourselves to Him and allowed Him to touch the areas of our most private pain and shame.

For Shelley to learn about the nature and causes of compulsivity was essential if she was to avoid her besetting sin.

Paul wrote to the Thessalonians, "[Let] each of you know how to possess his own vessel in sanctification and honor, not in lustful passion, like the Gentiles who do not know God" (1 Thessalonians 4:4-5). There it is again: The knowledge of God involves self-awareness. When a Christian is thus relieved of guilt and shame, he feels relief from anxiety. Not only does God know him, but he knows himself. He is not conscious of holding back anything from the Lord. This is the purest form of trust—to allow yourself to be known by God without fear.

In order to develop and maintain close relationships (which are crucial to successful living), we must have self-awareness—a right perception of ourselves with our weaknesses and strengths. Until we do, we will have difficulty disclosing ourselves to others and developing healthy relationships, or even rising to our own level of ability.

Shelley was vulnerable to temptation because she did not know herself. Had she been willing to let the Lord show her not only His salvation but insights about her compulsive personality, she would have been able to grow. But because she was unwilling to look at herself, she was unable to evaluate how the enemy had taken advantage of her weakness. She remained in the darkness of denial.

Self-awareness generally comes to a person who desires to know his or her true standing before God and with others. Until a person overrides his sense of shame and fear and comes out of hiding, he will be unable to see himself clearly. And to do this he must open up the blind side of his life to others.

Seeing the Blind Side

We all have a blind side. One way to see it is to interact with others and observe their blind sides. Ron, a sales manager in our congregation, asked his sales force what they noticed initially about their clients. The bald-headed men always noticed when their clients were bald. The overweight salesmen noticed weight. A good way to gain insight into our own blind side is to think of the flaws we notice in others. What behavior do we generally dislike in them? This little exercise can increase self-awareness.

Another way to increase self-awareness is to ask ourselves the question God asked of Cain: "Why are you angry? And why has your countenance fallen?" (Genesis 4:6). Discovering the roots of anger opens our blind side to revelation.

We might also ask God why we are vulnerable repeatedly to a certain temptation. In a recent prayer meeting with several pastors, one confessed that he had made repeated angry denunciations from the pulpit. But it became apparent that he was unaware of the reasons he was prone to do this. Until he understands the reasons, he is destined to repeat them.

Yet another way to discover our blind side is to seek out Christian counseling. But not everyone who seeks counseling is really looking to be known; many are simply looking for another spiritual activity. This does not substitute for self-awareness. Only when we are ready to see our blind sides will it do us any good to receive counseling.

The problems many Christians have faced for years have been healed only superficially by our inability to be self-aware. Rather than exhort others continually to be holy and cleansed, we are more likely to experience cleansing ourselves when we own up to the real reasons for the weaknesses that lead us to sin. Breakdowns in relationships go unheeded because, while we recognize the breach in a relationship, we do not realize the reason behind it.

Is it our denial that requires those around us to play our game of self-deceit? Is it the dysfunctional rigidity that developed in our home of origin, causing us to be exacting in our expectations of other Christians? So long as we cover the trouble spot with spiritual-sounding fig leaves, calling it something other than what it is, we walk in darkness because we are afraid to be self-aware.

Although Shelley had been a Christian for thirteen years, she knew little about herself and nothing of her blind side. She did not understand that her emotional wounds from childhood had a direct bearing on her current problem. And while she cannot blame others in the past for her present sin, she can realize that her anger over these wounds is a hidden force affecting her present choices.

Self-Acceptance

Once we see our weaknesses, we must acknowledge them for what they are. Discovering the reasons we have chosen to sin is crucial to getting free. We also need to accept the fact that perhaps for the rest of our lives this is the place where we are "temptable." Self-awareness must give way to self-acceptance. When we learn to love ourselves, flaws and all, we maintain a healthy respect for the passions that can drive us. A person who cannot accept his weaknesses moves quickly into denial, denying (among other things) the fact that sin has the power to overcome him. In reality, accepting weakness is not to give in to it or to condone it, but to learn to live with it and avoid the kinds of temptations that prey upon it.

Shelley needed to know her weakness with men in order to extricate herself from situations in which she would be tempted to intimacy with them. To keep herself from temptation, she needed to understand her anger toward her father and her insatiable need for male approval. She chose, rather, to fight the awareness of her weakness as much as an alcoholic fights the knowledge of his alcoholism.

The preacher who always preaches against a certain sin is usually preaching against it in himself. The more strongly he denounces the sin, the greater his delusion that he is driving it out of his life, as though to denounce it is to conquer it. He cannot accept himself as imperfect. He separates his false image of himself, which must be perfect, from his true self, which is weak.

It was this struggle of the apostle Paul to recognize himself as regenerate and yet flawed that he refers to in Romans 7: " . . . For I am not practicing what I would like to do, but I am doing the very thing I hate. . . . If I am doing the very thing I do not wish, I am no longer the one doing it, but sin which dwells in me. I find then the principle that evil is present in me, the one who wishes to do good" (verses 15, 20-21).

For the wounded woman, as for Paul, recognizing personal vulnerability to sin and the reasons for it provides the way to freedom. It is impossible to safeguard the heart and mind from temptation without understanding how we can be tempted. And admitting our ability to be tempted makes us aware of our need for God's grace. When we need God's grace, we can both receive it and give it to others. The pathway to humility is becoming aware of and accepting our own weaknesses so that we may unmask ourselves to others without fear of rejection.

If we keep the healing nature of self-awareness and self-acceptance at bay, on the other hand, every relationship will be hurt. We will feel that we do not need God. We will become impatient with others. And toward ourselves we will harbor self-contempt.

Self-Contempt

In spite of all Shelley's efforts to blame Bert for her adultery, her conscience continued to bother her. This is what brought her to counseling. As she pushed the boat full of her own weaknesses away from shore, she fell into the sea of temptation.

Shelley had disliked herself from childhood, particularly because of her father's lack of acceptance. Because she respected him, she reasoned that his opinions, including his apparent dislike for her, must be correct. She must be flawed. Now, as an adult, she hated how she looked and what she had become.

Ever trying to build her self-esteem, she looked to others to fill the void. When no other source of stimulation could fill it, Shelley was filled instead with self-contempt. Self-contempt leads ultimately to some form of self-sabotage—in Shelley's case, a particularly insidious form. Adultery robs a woman of confidence before God by multiplying her shame and leading her to commit more acts that will violate her conscience and destroy everything around her.

Unhealed emotional wounds, moreover, will embitter any individual. And according to the writer of Hebrews, the "root of bitterness" has the ability to defile many (12:15). The bitterness of Shelley's alcoholic father embittered her. Her unhealed emotional wounds led to her adultery, which in turn led to her husband's bitterness and the bitterness of her children.

Sad to say, Shelley abandoned her husband and children to pursue the adulterous relationship with Lou. Shelley's self-contempt led her to sabotage her happiness permanently.

What Could Have Saved Her?

Self-awareness and self-acceptance could have brought Shelley to the place of healing. She could have benefited from counseling and support group therapy as well as prayers for healing and freedom. But something else might have helped her. One other factor missing from Shelley's life was the intervention of her husband.

Bert, wanting to be an affirming husband and having no reason to believe Shelley would ever be unfaithful, raised no red flags when he noticed that she was devoting a disproportionate amount of time to her new pursuit. As is usually true, those closest to the addicted remain in denial about the severity of their addicted loved one's problem. And once Bert woke up to the fact that Shelley's affections had been transferred to another man, her addiction was greater than his ability to stop it.

Bert had every right to protect his relationship with his wife by setting boundaries. Marriage vows are intended to set boundaries for the relationship; and when the actions of either party seriously threaten those vows, the offended spouse should call it to the other's attention.

Particularly in the case of compulsive people (because they lose sight of boundaries), those close to them have the right and responsibility before God to help define and enforce those boundaries, to protect their loved ones and so that their own lives are not invaded with evil. Our rights stop where the rights of another are invaded. Had Bert called Shelley's activities into question the first time he noticed them, the exertion of that small amount of pressure might have been enough to jolt Shelley back to reality.

Bert's problem was the opposite of the husband who reacts with jealous outbursts in innocent situations. He went to the other extreme by continuing to deny that his wife was becoming involved emotionally with someone in the choir.

There is only one kind of person the grace of God cannot touch—the person unaware of his need for it. The wounded woman must know her limitations if she is to escape further wounding.

Let me add a postscript here. It is one thing to read this book and learn about emotional wounds, and quite another to implement the changes suggested. But until the wounded woman becomes self-aware, self-accepting and self-disclosing—to God and to other healthy Christians—she will continue as a sheep straying from her heavenly Father's care. If you are one of these women, why not open yourself now to God's gracious power to save you from the consequences of your own ways?

If you are in this position, you may wonder if the woman who has fallen is welcome back in the house of God. The Old Testament story of the conquest of Jericho highlights a woman named Rahab, a harlot whose brothel was a permanent fixture on the wall of Jericho. She and her house would have fallen when the walls fell, except for the fact that Rahab shielded the spies Moses had sent. Rahab made them promise that when they took Jericho, she and her whole household would be saved. As a sign Rahab hung a scarlet cord from her window— a cord that has come to symbolize the blood of Jesus Christ. When Jericho fell, Rahab's house was saved.

But the story does not end there. What happened to her? Rahab's life was changed by that experience. She became the mother of Boaz, the kinsman-redeemer who married Ruth. Rahab was part of the ancestry of Jesus Christ, a testimony of God's power not only to save but to restore. Jesus Christ, fully aware of His lineage, did not condemn the woman caught in adultery, but extended the same healing hand to her as He did to the blind and lame.

He offers the same cleansing power to us.

If you are like Shelley, you may never have understood the nature of your wounds and how they have led you into temptation. Now that you do, don't just confess adultery to the Lord, but open your life to the healing touch of Jesus at the roots of your compulsivity, your emotional wounds. Healing for you will likely not be a quick fix but a slow process as you disclose yourself to others. But the healing of these wounds will make the difference in your finding the path to righteousness.

We have seen the destructive power of relationships and of our own unhealed wounds. Let's look now at how God can use a Christian friend to help restore a woman who suffers what is perhaps one of the deepest wounds of all.

10

. . . .

Blessed Are They that Mourn

"Hot and humid with sunshine, high of 98." Normal sultry weather for a North Carolina summer day.

Mary Tepper had left early that morning with a car full of women for Williamsburg for a much-needed women's retreat five hours away. She and Elliott were now nearly six weeks into the missionary furlough she had awaited eagerly for four years. A feeling of uneasiness swept through her, but how many times had she felt that?

Elliott's itinerary for the summer was filled with weekend visits to contributing churches in the South and as far north as Chicago and Pennsylvania. But this weekend would be different, a chance for him and his sons—David, Jonathan, Peter and Timothy—to be together before furlough became even more hectic than the field in Spain. Nag's Head, North Carolina, where they would spend the night, seemed a good haven for male bonding. The Toyota van was loaded with supplies for the weekend. Elliott decided to give sixteen-year-old David, the oldest of the four, who had just gotten his driver's license, his first adventure behind the wheel.

The van wound its way over the back roads between Wilmington and New Bern, North Carolina, through pine forests and fields of tobacco and corn now withered in the heavy heat. As David negotiated the turns, careful of the soft, sandy shoulders lining the two-lane blacktop road, Elliott read the first four psalms aloud to everyone. Then he passed around food from the ice chest and turned to adjust nine-year-old Timothy's seatbelt. Timothy was sound asleep.

Suddenly a loud thump disrupted the calm as the wheels of the van dropped over the blacktop on a curve and onto the soft, sandy shoulder. The top-heavy van rolled over into a nearby ditch, tumbling its precious contents into a panic-stricken pile of arms and legs. What seemed like minutes took only seconds. And when the van came to rest, Elliott, sure that everyone had survived what seemed to be a minor mishap, counted heads.

David, Jonathan and Peter were shaken but O.K. But beside the road Timothy lay motionless. Elliott knelt beside him, lifting his head and shoulders ever so gently, and through tears prayed a desperate prayer for mercy for his nine-year-old boy. Slowly Timothy's trademark grin spread across his upturned face; but within minutes his breathing labored to a stop.

The van had come to rest in front of the home of a Christian family who had already sent for paramedics. Timothy Tepper was rushed to the hospital in New Bern but never regained consciousness. It was July 19, 1991, five days before his tenth birthday.

This sudden turn of events tore out a piece of Mary Tepper's heart forever. I sat ten rows behind her at the funeral (attended by nearly a thousand people) wondering how such a thing could happen. Mary and I had been friends for more than twenty years and had seen the Lord turn our lives in different directions like spokes on a wheel. The door to foreign missions had closed to Bill and me, and we had entered the pastoral ministry instead. But that door had swung wide to Mary, who had never aspired to missions!

After several difficult but fruitful years in Mexico, she and Elliott had now stuffed their family of six into an apartment in one of Madrid's drug-infested barrios and begun a mission to mainline heroin addicts. (Eight years later, Centro Betel has a center in Madrid with several outlying farms, as well as centers in several major Spanish cities and in Ceuta.) Death was always near. Over eighty percent of the members of their church came to Christ already infected with the AIDS virus. Mary and Elliott had watched this insidious plague, like a ticking time bomb, repeatedly wipe out precious Christian friends.

But encountering such grief in her own family was something Mary never anticipated. At first she felt peaceful sorrow. It must have been God's will. There was nothing she could have done. She and Elliott talked openly of their sorrow.

In the weeks after the funeral a horde of well-wishers came through the doors of their rented house. The steady flow of visits and mail poured oil into the wound. But living without Timothy was strange. Not only had he been their youngest, but he had held a childlike admiration for Mary and Elliott, as though their missionary zeal were his own bright vision— and perhaps it was. Also, since their remaining three sons were old enough to require little nurturing, Mary had moved overnight into a new phase of motherhood.

Mary's Pain

Two days after the last strains of the funeral hymns had faded, while I was staying with Mary for a while, she first mentioned a nagging thought: "Melinda, for just a few minutes last night, I couldn't help feeling angry with God. . . . "

Maybe it was the emotional strain of grief on a human soul, the almost unbearable impact of sorrow. But Mary was moving quickly into the next phase of grief, descending into a tunnel of negative emotions. As her friend, I could not help following her.

Anger usually follows the shock and denial that numb the worst emotional pain. With Mary, the numbness wore off quickly, exposing a throbbing wound too gaping and vast for someone like me to touch. Although words flow out of me with ease on paper, I was deeply afraid that any of my well-intentioned remarks would drive in like spears and enlarge her wound.

"I know, Mary," I said. "It's normal to feel that way with what you've been through. I felt that way, too, when Pop died."

I remembered how my grief had gone untouched and brought me to a place where God's pleasure no longer mattered to me. I wanted to fight back, to let God know that what He had allowed had hurt me and that I no longer cared whether or not I served Him.

Now I wanted to help Mary get her anger out, to acknowledge it. I wanted to validate her feelings, let her know she was not weird and that—with me, at least—she did not have to act spiritual and wear a mask for her pain.

But a month later Mary had to go back to Spain with her wounds still gaping and her pain isolating her from others, many of whom did not want to venture far into a thought life too real and unconcealed. One by one she declined the solace of friends, losing herself in a cavern of depression.

Once she was back in Spain her letters came in an avalanche, sometimes two a day. There were days I thought Mary would lose her mind or end her life. And I feared that, in anger, she might push me away, too, and move onto a sea of isolation, letting no one, not even God, touch the pain.

Nearly a year would pass before Mary started to walk in cautious steps back toward the light. And in that time, only one thing would warm her heart—the unconditional acceptance of friends who allowed her the right to grieve.

The Right to Grieve

Being a pastor and pastor's wife for sixteen years has given
me a window on the pain of people that others rarely see. What
is masked in the pew is often revealed in the pastor's study. At
the same time, I notice the fear that many Christians have of
emotion. It is as though there are right and wrong ways to feel,
particularly if you have Christ within. And to feel "wrong" is to
warrant chastisement from yourself or others.

Feeling the usual emotions associated with grief is somehow "wrong," according to many Christians. And when the
powerful earthquake known as grief moves in on the soul, what
should be an accepted course of events becomes instead a
source of shame.

The Christian is supposed to know better than to cry too
loudly or say bad things about God who, as we all know, controls the events that govern our lives. Men are given even less
permission to let themselves go. "Big boys don't cry." Adults
who grew up in dysfunctional homes have the added fear that
once they let go of themselves and give in to grief, they may
start crying and be unable to stop. But the fear of showing emotions—especially ones we consider negative—can rob us and
others of the right to grieve.

When the death of a loved one or the painful reverses of
life intrude on our circumstances, the human will is suddenly
crossed with the will of another. And since God is the One
who could have fixed the problem, He is often the focus of our
anger. The more intimate our relationship with God, the more
betrayed we may feel by the One who was supposed to be there
in our hour of need.

Mary, the sister of Lazarus, had sat at the feet of Jesus touched deeply by His teaching, setting this opportunity above important obligations of chores and entertaining. Yet Mary was angry at Jesus when He failed to show up in time to save her brother from death. "If You had been here," she admonished Him, "my brother would not have died!"

In the early days of the charismatic renewal, much emphasis was placed on "making a good confession"—speaking something positive—regardless of trying circumstances. Expressing negative emotions was squelched rather than encouraged. Many testimonies focused on the miraculous removal of suffering, both physical and emotional. Some even talked about facing the death of a loved one without a tear, having had all traces of sorrow miraculously removed.

While I have no doubt this happened in certain instances, it is not the norm. And the Christian unprepared for emotional upheaval—whether from the death of a loved one or another devastating circumstance—is prone to feel surprised, abandoned by God and swallowed up by the torrential force of grief.

Not only does the Christian feel abandoned by God; she often stands condemned by those who do not readily allow the expression of grief. In the presence of the view that showing grief is a sign of unbelief, the grieving one is obliged to submerge anger, fear and uncontrollable periods of weeping behind a spiritual mask. Regardless of how the bereaved is hurting, she may feel that God and others expect a stunning spiritual performance that belies her true feelings. The minister who has lost his wife would hardly dare vent his emotions in front of people in his congregation. God's reputation, after all, must not be sullied!

But who created human beings with the power to feel, cry and be angry?

If death comes near you and you think it is unspiritual to let go of your composure or "give in" to grief, you must gulp down fear, swallow your anger and bury your emotions in a grave. Or if any negative event precipitates feelings of depression, the Christian woman is usually conditioned spiritually to deny herself the right to an emotionally healthy response. Losing the right to *feel*, her sense of propriety is manipulated with Scripture, pressuring her into a facade of spirituality in which she cannot disclose her true self. Whether because she might lose her testimony or even her own fellowship with God, the sensitive Christian woman fears she has no right to exercise her emotions, to grieve normally.

Each person has a built-in inhibitor serving as a barrier to "uncivilized" behavior. But when grief traverses the boundaries we feel are legal, we subconsciously move (without realizing it) to enforce those boundaries. And we enforce them not only on ourselves but on those around us. In a subconscious effort to stifle grief reactions in others that make us feel uncomfortable, for example, we resort to trite-sounding scriptural admonitions or what we feel are soothing words. Our acts of consolation are actually attempts to remove a person's right to grieve.

Mary Tepper learned quickly about the unhealthy expectations of other Christians. Some, in an effort to console her, almost pushed her back into her hole of private grief as a child would a jack-in-the-box. Perhaps their own fears of dying or grieving or losing a child—or perhaps the dysfunctional inability to show emotion—made them uncomfortable. They offered to bring her pain to a speedy conclusion because to prolong it heightened their own discomfort.

Perhaps the worst mistakes were made by those attempting to find some meaning in Timothy's death so that Mary could stop grieving and "go on with God." Phrases like "God knows best" and "Your ministry will only be more powerful now" offered little comfort. How much did she, in her pain, care about ministry opportunities if her son had to give his life? (Besides, Jesus Christ's sacrifice for sin atoned for our salvation

because no other's could have.) Was it intended to be comforting for Mary to follow that line of reasoning and infer that
God had checked a list of potential victims that day, selected
the ones who needed to die and decided that Timothy should
be among them?

If these comments were thought through to their roots,
they would be found to have no basis in Scripture—not to mention that they hurt a grieving mourner's relationship with God.

Some Christians shared their testimonies of how the Lord
brought them through the death of a child. But the majority
reacted strangely. Within a few weeks Mary was receiving cards
full of chit-chat, either not mentioning Timothy or sandwich-
ing in a glib sentence or two between talk about summer vacation. Some of Mary and Elliott's associates have yet to mention Timothy's name, apparently hoping that ignoring the
event means it did not happen and that things can go on as
usual.

But Jesus put His heart into people, like the Good Samaritan, that Mary never expected. A Christian woman from Com-
passionate Friends writes her every month from the U.S., walking with her through her pain, willing to listen to her thoughts
(which many Christians would consider bizarre, if not down-
right wicked). One morning Mary opened her door to an elderly
Spanish woman she barely knew from the neighborhood. She,
too, had lost a child. With no spiritual mask to uphold, the
woman wrapped Mary in her arms and sobbed with her.

A Safe Place

The woman experiencing feelings she sees as shameful desperately needs an atmosphere in which these feelings can be
vented and validated. The woman who needs to share the
tragedy of a failed marriage, the torment of abuse, the pain of
living with an alcoholic, the worry for a backsliding child, the

disappointment of a barren womb, will not feel free to speak up when she knows her feelings will be perceived as invalid or "unspiritual." Unfortunately, Christian groups are often rigid regarding what feelings or experiences they validate and those they do not. Just as some communities espouse only views that are academically or "politically correct," so do some churches espouse only views that are "spiritually correct."

Job experienced this dilemma when he vented his frustration and anger over his loss and his feelings of victimization at the hands of God. He was visited by friends with "spiritually correct" views based on the concept of a God who rewards good and punishes evil—carried to legalistic lengths.

When Job lost his children and possessions as well as his health, he concluded that he as a righteous man was being punished unfairly by God. His friends reinforced the belief that God always punishes evil—Job must, therefore, have sinned, they said—and they admonished him to stop complaining. He should be more "spiritual" and have more spiritually correct views—as though he could separate from his pain and adjust his theology.

Job's primary stressor turned out to be his legalistic theology. His friends were unwilling to validate his pain because to do so would open them up to the possibility of unexplained suffering in their own lives.

The Church is often like this today, frightened of acknowledging unexplained suffering while denying those in pain the right to grieve without being condemned by self-righteous judgments. How we ought to feel is not what God wants us to acknowledge. Instead, acknowledging how we really feel is the first step in self-disclosure that gives rise to a revelation of God to us.

Let's examine the words of Jesus.

Blessed Are They that Mourn

No one was more disgusted than Jesus with the legalistic belief system established by the Pharisees. His simple teachings, cutting through their religiosity and false spirituality, invited all who had been distanced from God by having to adopt "spiritually correct" views and disclose only "correct" feelings to step into God's approval.

In the Beatitudes Jesus established the expression of need and weakness as the basis for experiencing a revelation of God. "Blessed are they that mourn" is the initial step of self-disclosure that reassures such people that "they shall be comforted" (Matthew 5:4, KJV).

The word for *comfort* is a form of *parakaleo* in Greek that means "the one who stands alongside." It is the word Jesus used to describe to the disciples the coming of the Holy Spirit, the Comforter or Helper. In order to draw on the Helper, the believer must ask for help or simply disclose his need for help. Open mourning is a form of self-disclosure. No longer do men and women have to hide from God, covering their shame with fig leaves of denial. Instead, exposing the areas they feared to reveal brings a sense of closeness to God and even strengthens them with divine enablement.

The apostle Paul reiterated this truth when he wrote that Jesus Christ's strength was perfected in his own weakness, "for when I am weak, then am I strong" (2 Corinthians 12:10, KJV). Only when a woman discloses to the Lord the shocking depths of her pain and sorrow can she experience the real comfort of the Holy Spirit.

Providing a Safe Atmosphere

Only when a woman trusts will she disclose herself. So in all our relationships and churches, providing an atmosphere for the deepest self-disclosure is all-important. Otherwise, the members of the Body of Christ will seek this atmosphere elsewhere.

I met a friend in the grocery store recently whom I have known off and on for more than fifteen years. It seemed a providential meeting because Charlotte never shopped there and I never shopped there at that time of day. The conversation moved to what we were currently involved in. I told her about my two books on addiction in the Church and dysfunctional families.

Then she blurted out a secret she had never divulged in any of our previous conversations. Her Christian son is an alcoholic. When she felt that I would accept her, knowing of her alcoholic son and approving of his seeking help in Alcoholics Anonymous, she felt safe to disclose her area of private pain. She also said her son had told her repeatedly, "Mom, the church didn't help me. A.A. helped me."

Why? Because in the churches he had attended, there was no safe atmosphere of self-disclosure in which his struggle with the addictive cycle could be exposed and validated as real, *apart from* his struggle with God and the devil. Had he disclosed his alcoholism, he might have been shamed as being infected with evil rather than validated as a Christian struggling with addictive cravings proceeding from a physical and emotional—not spiritual—root.

Sometimes we are afraid that if we validate pain in others, we will seem to condone it and give them permission to sin. Actually the opposite is true. After Adam and Eve sinned, God sought to cover their shame lovingly rather than expose it. But He could not dress them in garments of skin until the fig leaves they were using to conceal their nakedness had been acknowledged and removed. In Christ the believer who exposes his or her weakness is clothed with divine love that mends the damage done in Eden.

When Paul wrote, "Rejoice with those who rejoice, and weep with those who weep" (Romans 12:15), he was exhorting the Church to a new level of intimacy, to become a place where not only joy but pain can be exposed and experienced together.

It was this kind of atmosphere that Mary Tepper was looking for and could not (with a few exceptions) find. Fellow believers either refused to validate her, ignoring her pain; required that she get rid of her pain as soon as possible; insisted she find meaning behind the accident—for example, that God had allowed Timothy's death to further His Kingdom; or compelled her to draw obvious spiritual conclusions, agree that God is good and put the pain behind her.

Why *did* Timothy die? I do not know. No one can know this side of heaven. What we do know is that God promises, upon our arrival in the heavenly house, to take us in His arms and wipe away our tears. Whether the tears are symbolic of the trials of this life or actual tears associated with pain and death, the Father promises to heal broken hearts (whether here on earth or there in heaven). How does He do it?

Ruth

The ancient story of Ruth's steadfast love for her mother-in-law, Naomi, illustrates the power of a friend's validation in times of emotional pain. The first chapter of Ruth (which we looked at in chapter 3) records Naomi's deep sense that the deaths of her husband and sons were signs of God's punishment, probably for leaving Bethlehem and seeking refuge from famine in Moab, a country God unconditionally rejected. She assumed that if her daughters-in-law, Ruth and Orpah, returned to Bethlehem with her, nothing would await them but sorrow and the rejection of being foreigners. So she encouraged them to leave her to her grief. In fact, she practically pushed them away.

But Ruth refused to leave. The expression of her commitment to Naomi in the face of a bleak future is often quoted at weddings: "Do not urge me to leave you or turn back from following you; for where you go, I will go, and where you lodge, I will lodge. Your people shall be my people, and your God, my God. Where you die, I will die, and there I will be buried" (Ruth 1:16-17).

Many see Boaz as the only type of Christ in this book. But Ruth, whose name means "friendship," also foreshadows the One who is "a friend who sticks closer than a brother" (Proverbs 18:24), Jesus Christ, who promises never to forsake us. His love is unconditional and unwavering even in the midst of our grief, anger and distorted perception of God. While Naomi grieved, Ruth sought food and restoration for the mother-in-law to whom she had committed herself for life.

What God wants in the Church today are friends like Ruth who will allow Naomis torn with sorrow, disappointment and grief to vent their spiritually incorrect feelings and maintain their love, commitment and even approval. This is no codependent commitment, but one based on the understanding that my validation of my sister's suffering provides one avenue of healing, one puzzle piece in the plan of God for my friend's restoration.

In our willingness to listen without judgment to her expressions of anger and disappointment, we add a dimension of Christlikeness to our own character and provide an atmosphere for self-disclosure for our friend, thus helping her to experience Jesus Christ, the restorer of mourners.

Jesus Attends a Funeral

When Jesus arrived four days late at the tomb of Lazarus, one of His closest friends, the house was surrounded with mourners questioning His failure to interrupt His friend's suffering with a miracle. Martha expressed faith, but her sister, Mary, grieving the loss of their brother, Lazarus, reacted differently. She spoke with bitterness of soul to Jesus.

Making His way to the tomb, Jesus entered the pathos of the moment. In an act that disclosed not only His humanity but the feelings of God over the deaths of men and women, the Scripture says simply that "Jesus wept" (John 11:35).

Many have supposed that He wept over their unbelief. But His tears carried one message to the Jews: "Behold how He loved him!" (verse 36). Even the hardhearted Pharisees associated Jesus' tears with His love. I am sure that is the conclusion God wants us to draw.

Jesus did not expect Mary to generate more faith. He was and is the embodiment of faith. He did not act religious or super-spiritual. He just cried, loudly enough for everyone to hear. Then He raised Lazarus from the dead. So Mary's mourning gave way to a revelation of Jesus' resurrection power: "Blessed are they that mourn, for God Himself shall come and stand beside them."

How can I be more like Jesus in my ministry to grieving friends? How can I help restore wounded women?

What to Do and Say

The ministrations most remembered by hurting people involve not words but actions that stop and salute the moment, respecting the feelings of the grieving for life to stop, if only for a bit. The day of my father's funeral, the garbage man came as usual. It hurt me to see that life kept going and no one noticed or cared. *How can you be taking out the garbage*, I thought, *when my father has died?*

So, first, *Stop what you are doing to enter your friend's grief.* This will speak volumes.

Chuck, a retired banking executive in our church, recalls from his boyhood the funeral of his uncle. As the funeral procession wound through town and to the cemetery, an elderly black gentleman saw the procession, stopped what he was doing, removed his hat and placed it over his heart, standing at attention until they had all passed by. The mental picture of that moment has remained with Chuck for over fifty years: a stranger caring enough to show respect.

Do not say, "I know how you feel," unless you have suffered the same problem or grieved the loss of the same relationship— a father, a spouse, a child. Even then, every problem is unique. And with a death, the world has lost a person who will not pass this way again. Simply saying, "I'm sorry" is far better than trying to put yourself in the grieving person's place.

It is better not to be "religious" and look for ways to balance the equation of pain and suffering, as Job's friends did. We always err when we look for a positive or negative reason behind someone's suffering or death. These are part of life, and trying to figure out why God touches one and takes another does untold damage and hurt. Nor should we draw a line between one's shortcomings and one's death. When our own precious ones die, we will only have heaped condemnation on our heads.

Do not tell your friend how much better she will feel later or how great her ministry will be when the crisis is past. She cannot see past her pain and may not care two hoots right now about her ministry. What she cares about is knowing that her loved one was loved and appreciated.

Let your grieving friend talk about her loved one. One of the couples who came to console Mary and Elliot were Douglas and Margaret Feaver, a retired college professor and his wife who are now missionaries themselves. Douglas and Margaret lost their three-year-old son to encephalitis more than thirty years ago. Margaret advises allowing the bereaved to talk about the deceased. Tears may come and you will probably cry, too. But there is no higher compliment you can pay a grief-stricken person than crying with her over her loss. It is what Jesus did.

Do not quote Scriptures and offer teachings about what has helped you, unless she asks specifically. One well-meaning person gave Mary a tape by a well-known teacher who advised the grieving to lay aside their sorrow and praise the Lord for a period of three hours. This, he promised, would make the pain go away. All such words as these will be hollow as you shove off on the grieving your "hidden agenda," which usually deprives them of their right to grieve in their own way. "I just can't praise the Lord," Mary told me through tears, "Not yet, anyway."

Remember that every person grieves differently, according to his or her own temperament, tradition and emotional conditioning. Recent figures indicate that more than eighty percent of couples who lose a child wind up in divorce. It is generally believed that each spouse expects the other to grieve the loss in the same way. Rather than console each other, they wind up trying to squeeze the spouse into their own mold.

Margaret Feaver says that it took about a year for the pain of the memory of her son's death to leave. One morning she awoke to the knowledge that the awful pain was gone. What took Margaret a year may take another less, or much longer. Healing comes at an individual's own pace. Keep giving your friend the privilege of tears and talk when she wants to.

Continue to assure her of your love and acceptance even when she discloses spiritually incorrect feelings. This helps her share her worst feelings and feel accepted. There is no greater treasure than a friend who knows all about you and loves you anyway. If this is how we want God to treat us, then let us treat our suffering or grieving friend the same way.

If we allow our Christian friends the right to grieve any loss in this manner, whether it is small or great, we will provide the necessary atmosphere in our relationship for self-disclosure. As we are healed of our own codependency, we will no longer feel the need to adjust the other person, but will come to the place in which we can trust the Lord to reveal Himself to our friend as she expresses her deepest hurts.

The truth of sowing and reaping applies here. When it is our own turn to grieve, we will be more likely to find the same accepting shoulder to cry on and the freedom to work through our own pain without the threat of the condemnation of others.

The following poem, "Save with a Friend" by Dinah Craik, describes how a grieving person feels with a true, validating friend:

> O, the comfort, the inexpressible comfort of feeling safe with a
>   person,
> Having neither to weigh thoughts, nor measure words,
> But pouring them right out, just as they are,
> Chaff and grain together,
> Certain that a faithful hand will take and sift them,
> Keep what is worth keeping,
> And with the breath of kindness blow the rest away.

Once we in the Church are committed to providing a safe atmosphere for self-disclosure, we will come far closer to restoring the wounded, battle-weary victims of warfare.

But what is it that puts an end to shame and anger and removes us permanently from the roller coaster of hope and disappointment? Let's read on.

11

The Death of a Dream

Whether it is the dream of having a happy marriage, rearing children who serve God, even being able to have children, the dream itself can become our greatest source of pain. It can become the basis for comparing reality against an illusion that will never be God's will for us. I do not intend in this chapter to destroy real hope but false hope, and help you recognize the difference.

False hope for many Christians masquerades as faith, as we wrap our illusion in clouds of denial. More people have died from denial than from the disease itself; while they wait for the symptoms to disappear and the harsh reality of serious illness to fade into an illusion of health that never comes.

In a painful act of public self-disclosure, I will illustrate this chapter with the death of a dream I have had for a long time.

My Own Dream

For sixteen years Bill and I have ministered together at the Church of the Risen Saviour. But if you had told me this more than a decade and a half ago—when we first viewed the city of Pittsburgh from Mount Washington, let our eyes scan its rivers and valleys and claimed it for the Gospel—I would have rebuked you for your unbelief!

I came here with Bill quite against my personal preference, leaving my home state of Texas with its black-eyed peas, cornbread and the anxious pleas of my Aunt Bessie: "Oh, hon, you don't want to go up tha-yur!" Indeed, I did not. Who wanted to live in a place where the temperature is still in the 20s in April? But I was willing to suffer for the Gospel even if it meant gutting it out until victory came!

Bill and I had been members of Beverly Hills Baptist Church in Dallas and had just witnessed a three-year period during which the church had mushroomed from 800 members to over 6,000. It was a revival unlike any I have seen before or since. And I fully expected God to use Bill and me to make it happen in Pittsburgh's inner city.

We came to a church with fewer than fifteen active members who were recovering from the devastation of watching their founding pastor publicly reveal his homosexuality and plunge headlong into the gay rights movement. But we were undaunted in our expectations and saw this challenge as fuel for God's redemptive flame. Having seen what God could do, we believed it was only a matter of time (although we knew we would endure a testing of our faith) before we would see our vision fulfilled: a large church in full swing with every ministry in place.

We were there only six weeks when our denomination noticed we were of charismatic persuasion, something we had never concealed, and cut off financial support. Our baby daughter, Sarah, was only one year old when the financial rug was pulled out from under her starry-eyed parents, but God never let us fall. The church in Dallas quickly organized a mission board to provide us with some monthly support. Although we lived in poor neighborhoods and under conditions some would have considered rough, we did not miss paying a bill or eating a meal. To this day I do not know how.

But in spite of financial provision, the church struggled. We found a church building in inner-city Pittsburgh vacant on Sundays where we could meet. We absorbed ourselves in church work and "work days" waiting for the day God would "move." Knowing little about running a church, we had to muddle our way through. We wound up appointing all the wrong people to leadership positions, only to see the church divide several times over conflicts that bruised our emotions and for a season quenched our faith. But even these obstacles could not push us off the ground we knew God had given us.

The people we attracted in the city were not, for the most part, yuppies but a biracial, multi-ethnic congregation of single adults without jobs, single-parent victims of divorce, college students, street people and a few token "normal" families. We tried with a small budget to support foreign missions, invite guest speakers and hold evangelistic outreaches. We continued to expect God to move. We also got encouragement from one guest minister after another that an outpouring of the Holy Spirit was just over the horizon.

Bill and I (long forsaken by the denomination in which I had grown up) were ordained in 1982 at Evangelistic Center in Kansas City, Missouri, a fellowship of Full Gospel churches. At our ordination, we were encouraged to continue to expect a move of God.

Three years later the rented building in which we were meeting was torn down. But God opened for us, through a providential turn of events, a lovely Gothic stone and stained-glass church building as if to reward us for suffering in the ruin we used to call a church building in the inner city.

We have been here ever since. Surges of growth have come and gone. Each season of growth seems to be cut short when people we have poured our lives into look for churches in which everything smells new, the worship is more professional and all the programs are in place. Part of me left along with each one. Some of them never really learned how much we loved them because they could not love themselves. But when we lose contact, their faces live in my memory with the remembrances of laughter and tears when we served God together. And with each departure, as the years wore on and the fulfillment of my dream was not forthcoming, my shame increased.

What I am saying, then, is that I know what it means to want something for years and grieve through the hills and valleys of the hope/disappointment roller coaster. For yoked to this dream of mine, as it is for every other person who owns a dream like this, has always been my sense of worth.

God has blessed Bill and me in thousands of ways less public but sometimes more important. But the cry of Hannah, "Give me children lest I die," always tugged at my fragile emotions and longed for fulfillment. I have gone through periods when I did not care if my dream was ever fulfilled, periods I was sure I had let go of any wrong motive behind the dream. But sooner or later the dying embers of hope in me would burn red-hot with zeal once again.

Any woman who has held onto the tiniest shred of faith in any heartfelt desire amid a difficult tempest knows the gamut of emotions I have described. Regardless of the dream, the emotional ups and downs are the same. And so is the result—distraction from other pursuits that are more likely to be the will of God, or else spiritual and emotional burnout.

I can imagine how Abraham and Sarah must have felt to hold onto God's promise of a son for more than twenty years. Self-doubt gnaws at you as you dig in your soul to find the hidden sin or problem blocking God's blessing. I cannot criticize Abraham and Sarah for wanting to take matters into their own hands. I have felt the very same temptation.

And after sixteen years I have analyzed not only my dream but the dreams of many who have been devastated on the hope/disappointment roller coaster. In order to get off the roller coaster, we must take a long, hard look at how we boarded the ride. Let's examine seven factors that make a dream unhealthy.

Seven Qualities of an Unhealthy Dream

In the beginning an unhealthy dream may seem harmless or even good. The desire to parent, for example, is a healthy desire God puts in the human race to keep us going. Having a husband is a normal desire, too, as are getting into the right college and succeeding in your career.

But the question is not whether the dream in general is godly. The question is, is it God's will for you personally? Every dream that keeps a woman on the hope/disappointment roller coaster *seems* viable. But as time wears on and the dream remains unfulfilled, an unhealthy dream causes painful results. Check each blank in the following listing that applies to your own dream:

_____ 1. Does holding onto my dream cause me to maintain a pervasive sense of dissatisfaction with my present circumstances, which are really beyond my control?

It is impossible to be happy as long as you feel that your present is less than it should be, or unacceptable. In order for the dreamer to be happy, the unhealthy dream must be fulfilled. A woman with an unhealthy dream usually has an underlying anxiety propelling her forward, so that any sense of satisfaction about the present is short-lived. It is as though she jumps the high bar to the best of her ability, only to see it raised again just beyond reach.

_____ 2. Does holding onto my dream make me unable to accept the present as God's will for me?

The feeling that we are out of God's will somehow gets us back on track when we have sinned, but it is a lousy thermometer for directional guidance. One of Satan's chief tricks is making us feel we have missed it—even just a little bit. Under performance-based Christianity, of course, if we have missed it even by a little bit, our dream will not come to pass and we will be driven from God's best for our lives.

_____ 3. Does holding onto my dream give me a sense of urgency to adjust my performance or actions in order to earn God's blessing?

Think hard. The woman dissatisfied with the present is usually engaged in feverish, draining activity, either to assure herself that she is doing her part in God's plan, or to quench her doubt that her dream is really from God. The Parable of the Talents, in which each man was given a different number of talents, makes this busy woman feel uneasy. *Am I doing all I can*, she asks, *to ensure that God will reward my stewardship?* Rather than try to increase her capacity to love, this woman (because of her unhealthy goals) focuses on visible performance that she feels will be visibly rewarded.

_____ 4. Do I have a sense of shame or embarrassment that my dream has not yet come to pass, that it seems to elude my grasp?

Whenever the fulfillment of the dream is not forthcoming, the unhealthy dreamer begins to develop a sense of rejection by God because it has not happened. This feeling of shame often increases when those around the dreamer appear to be blessed in precisely the way she feels she should be blessed, while she continues to struggle.

_____ 5. Do I feel angry with God or others that my dream has not been fulfilled, as though God or someone else is at fault for prolonging it or sabotaging its fulfillment?

The story of Joseph in the Old Testament should be enough to tell every believer that regardless of how men try to snuff out a godly vision, it will come to pass anyhow in God's timing. But anger with God and others erupts if we believe they have the power to take our dream away or sabotage its fulfillment.

_____ 6. Is my sense of self-worth tied to the fulfillment of my dream? If it comes to pass, will I feel rewarded for my accomplishments or great faith or having "paid my dues," enduring through awful situations?

The presence of an unhealthy dream, when its fulfillment is not forthcoming, causes me to feel bad about myself or about my natural or spiritual gifts.

_____ 7. Am I afraid to let go of my dream for fear of displaying a lack of faith that may keep the dream from coming to pass?

Holding onto an unhealthy dream may be causing painful or destructive consequences in your own life or in the lives of others. Many a woman holds onto the false hope that her alcoholic or otherwise abusive husband will get the message through her passive behavior. Taking any steps she believes might jeopardize his salvation or bring a breakthrough in the situation is out of the question, since she is afraid of incurring the wrath of God, worse heartache, the loss of the dream (e.g., her husband's salvation) or even the loss of her own salvation.

Whenever you believe that losing faith in your dream will cause the Lord to treat you with disfavor, losing the dream is the best thing that can happen to you. Then you will find out that God's love for you does not depend on your ability to believe in it.

What creates an unhealthy dream with any or all of the above consequences? Look over your own life to see how your false hope was created.

Creating False Hope

There are many means the enemy uses—our emotional wounds, our pride, even our well-meaning Christian friends—to create false hope. Let's look at four ways this happens.

The first way is *when we compare our situation negatively with others*. Somehow we tend to believe, particularly in affluent Western civilization, that everyone is entitled to equal opportunities and privileges. We may feel jealous when we see a sister blessed or prospered in an area in which we are experiencing lack.

Yet all of our lives reveal different forms of blessing. One family may be prosperous financially while another enjoys better health. The problem arises when we try to play God, fix our hope on the outcome of a particular prayer and read hidden meaning into it when it does not happen.

Accepting the apparent prosperity of others in areas where we struggle is easier when we take an honest look at other factors that may have contributed to their success. Perhaps it is not a matter of supernatural favor at all, but of natural ability, timing, earlier choices or other factors. Maybe one company led the way in a particular area or improved on a particular method. Whatever the case, we should not feel inferior, and certainly not condemned. Perhaps we can even improve on someone else's improvements! But feeling that God's blessing is somehow linked to someone in a way that it is not linked to us only produces condemnation and another valley on the hope/disappointment roller coaster.

Another factor contributing to the development of false hope comes *when we adopt a success model different from God's will for our lives.* Reading slick, four-color magazines full of how-to's impossible to implement at our own level of development or financial ability only creates discouragement. It is O.K. not to read these publications!

In the Body of Christ, for example, we have certain models for successful church ministers that may impair our ability to accept our own minister as an individual. These amount to unrealistic expectations. What happens, for example, when our minister falls far short of perfection? When his personality and giftings are different from our own, or from those of the last minister? When God leads him in a different direction than the congregation expects?

Which brings up the next problem that creates false hope: *when we allow the well-intentioned but uninspired words of others to help create our illusion and perpetuate our false hope.* Later we will be shocked into hard, cold reality. In some circles, one of the gifts of the Holy Spirit, the gift of prophecy, has been abused to create false hope. I have been edified by prophecy and have seen it operate in many different forms, even through people who did not believe in it or did not know they were prophesying. But I have also had grandiose things prophesied about me that would have shipwrecked me had I not judged them by Scripture, discerned the spirit behind the messages and compared them with other things I felt the Lord had said to me.

Recall the time Peter took Jesus aside and told Him He would never suffer and be killed. Jesus did not allow Peter's exuberance and what amounted to no more than well wishes—"man's interests," Jesus called them (Matthew 16:23)—to create an illusion that would distract Him from His mission.

Finally, false hope creates an illusion *whenever it is substituted for God's faith*. Dr. Charles Price, the Pentecostal evangelist whose gifts of healing miracles were widely known in the first half of the twentieth century, wrote this in his classic book *The Real Faith*:

> There is a great deal of difference between what we call the faith of man in God, and the faith of God that is imparted to man. Such faith is not the child of effort, neither is it born of struggle. If it is the faith of God, then we get it from Him, and not from our mental attitudes or affirmations.

When a woman's hopes and dreams are not born of God's faith but have created an illusion, that illusion is destined to fail, bringing with it despair. Until her illusion is dead, God's true plan for her life will be obscured. And you cannot be happy where you are right now until you are dead to what *could* be.

But how can I let go of a dream I have held onto for years? Won't I be destroyed?

God will help you back to healthy faith by separating your hope in the illusion from your hope in Him. If you hold onto a dream that is not from God, your faith will be destroyed. But letting go of a God-authored dream will not affect its outcome because it has resurrection life of its own.

Letting Go

Letting go of a false dream will take a measure of God's power because you are probably holding it tightly. Seven steps lead to the death of false hope. Ask the Lord for His help in walking through them.

1. *Recognize and admit that you may have been deceived about the dream.* Even if your dream is from God, you may be unclear on how and when it is to occur. And by your trying to force God into your own mold, your dream may have become unhealthy. You may have put faith in something, even out of good intentions, that will never happen. Ask God to help you look at the possibility that it is a false hope. You need help to do this, since it is not possible without the grace of the Lord.

2. *Let the dream die by putting it to rest.* Refuse to entertain any thoughts that it will come to pass. Stop imagining yourself walking down the aisle, or holding the baby in your arms, or whatever your dream has been. Real dreams will come to pass without the help of your vivid imagination. But God will undoubtedly do beyond what you ask or think in another way you have not yet imagined.

3. *Enjoy the feeling of peace that comes when you do not have to have your dream fulfilled in order to continue to trust the Lord, feel loved by Him or approved by others.*

4. *Let yourself enjoy the present circumstances.* What if you do not live past tomorrow? Shouldn't you be able to enjoy God and others today? A pastor of a large church advised other ministers to enjoy their churches at their current stage of growth.

5. *Let go of anger you have held toward others you felt were inhibiting the fulfillment of your dream.* Julie approached me at a women's retreat, having prayed for years for a baby. Ever since she and her husband had discovered that he was infertile, she had harbored anger and unforgiveness toward him. Then I realized I held anger toward stubborn people who refused to

change. I had perceived them as threats to what I believed God had promised me and had seen them as short circuits to the fulfillment. Recognizing, admitting and letting go of resentment—which Julie and I both did—lets you accept and love others as part of God's will for you today. Rather than worthless, dead baggage, these people become precious.

6. *Let God define any future dreams or expectations.* Be wary that your vivid imagination or need for emotional validation has caused you to fall for encouraging words or false prophecies that have defined an unrealistic expectation of God's timing and/or purpose. Jesus promised that the Holy Spirit would bring to your remembrance whatever He had spoken. This has happened to me many times as God reminds me that present events are the fulfillment of things He has promised me in the past.

7. *Let God heal your emotional wounds so that your low self-esteem or martyr complex does not prevent God from using you in other ways different from the false dream you have held.* Healing from emotional wounds will also make you less vulnerable to false prophecy or forms of false encouragement that are merely well wishes in disguise.

Letting go of your dream may be the hardest thing you have ever done. But it is the gateway to seeing God's blessing in other ways and finding contentment and peace. Here is what happened to my dream.

The Death of My Dream

I did not understand what it meant to die to self—not really—until my sixteen years of private pain came to a head while I was teaching a retreat for another church in the area. The theme was "Taking Off Shame, Putting On Glory."

It was usually painful for me to teach a women's retreat for a group of happy, excited women at another church. Why would they want me to come teach their retreat when comparatively few people wanted to attend our church? And on this day I found myself particularly reluctant to teach on the barrenness syndrome, reluctant to bring up the subject in front of a group of women from another church. I feared that my private shame would surface, the shame I had faced over and over about the size of our church. Sixteen years of this experience were finally taking their toll.

Although Bill and I had had many assurances through other Christians that one day our church would grow, after sixteen years it was as small as ever. What's more, this particular retreat was attended by several women who had gone to our church for a few years and decided, for one reason or another, to leave. During the retreat itself one woman who had left four years before took me aside and, in an attempt to affirm me, told me how much she respected me for being willing to minister to "weird" people. Our congregation had undergone a transition since she had left, but I couldn't help wondering, *Is that how our church is characterized by others?* The shame was only increasing.

Back in my room I began to pace the floor.

"Lord, I have to have an answer," I prayed. "I can't go on like this."

I dotted my nails with polish and flopped down on the bed waiting for the moment when it would be my turn again to speak. In the deepest corner of my mind, the faintest voice whispered, *Not My will but Thine be done.*

"Oh, yes, Lord, I know I should say it, but I can't right now. But I'll try to find a way."

As the message progressed that afternoon, my voice broke several times at what I thought were inopportune moments. The women fell silent, as they usually do when I begin to describe the pain of unanswered prayer—a pain I knew all too well, and they did, too. What they did not know was that they were by their very presence causing me to feel that pain at that moment. I exhorted them to remove the shame of others by affirming those others at the very point of their shame.

I finished the message to the affirmation of hearty amens and a round of stirring applause and sat down.

The next morning back at my own church, our small, less enthusiastic crowd replaced the large, spiritually charged atmosphere of the retreat. It was Palm Sunday and Bill was preaching about Jesus' triumphal entry into Jerusalem and the crowd cheering Him, only to reject Him a few days later. As Bill spoke, his voice trailed into the background and the Lord's voice broke through to me: *You talk of My unconditional love for you and for others. Will you unconditionally love and accept Me?*

Light broke through. I had to accept the way the Lord chose to work in my life, the way He had disclosed Himself to Me, based not on what He could potentially do for me or for others, but on what He was willing to do for me now.

I thought about Shadrach, Meshach and Abednego in the book of Daniel as they were about to be cast into the fiery furnace. They knew God's ability but told King Nebuchadnezzar in a Spirit-inspired act of courage: "Our God whom we serve is able to deliver us from the furnace of blazing fire. . . . But even if He does not . . . we are not going to serve your gods or worship the golden image that you have set up" (Daniel 3:17-18).

They accepted God, negatives and positives, however He chose to disclose Himself. And once they had been thrown into the furnace, a fourth Man, whose appearance was "like a son of the gods" (verse 25), came and stood beside them. The fire that tested them had no effect.

I had to accept the Lord on the same basis: whether or not He ever made our church grow.

At 4:30 the next morning I had a dream sense that two dark figures were dragging me through the woods against my will to the brink of a hole they had dug for me. I eluded their grasp, escaping into the woods. Then I had the impression that this had happened several times, and each time they had found me and brought me back to the hole. Being buried alive with no hope of rescue had, in fact, been a childhood nightmare.

But instead of the presence of tormenting fear, suddenly the scene changed. The two dark figures were nailing Jesus to the cross and He was not trying to pull away. Calmly He allowed them to place Him there, drive the nails in and hoist Him above a crowd hurling insults and pouring shame on Him. But it was as though Jesus had already died. He offered no resistance. Nor did He seem to demonstrate the anger of a passive will acquiescing hopelessly to a situation thrust upon Him. He exuded peace in the middle of pain.

Jesus' power had come from His unanswered prayer in Gethsemane, I realized, the place where heaven was silent and the only sound was the swishing of olive trees in the night breeze and the snoring of the sleeping disciples who did not seem to care. Jesus had really died *there*. Though I had preached on it before, I had not really seen it until now.

This was it. My dream of pastoring a church (alongside my husband) of several hundred members engaged eagerly in following the Lord together would have to die. Not out of anger, but it would have to die. And along with it would go my independent will prone to wander from His. I would have to accept and trust His purpose unconditionally. I could not relish the fact that I was more spiritual, more holy or more crucified than anyone else. I am not. I would have to die and trust that around the fresh dirt heaped on the grave, new sprouts would come to life, the sprouts He wanted, not the ones I had dreamed and imagined.

I was not experiencing a codependent death of false martyrdom, and I understood at that moment the difference. It was all right to tell other women that God is not interested in unwarranted suffering. He is not looking for a woman whose private pain was to be beaten and abused by a vicious man, convulsing daily in the throes of death without ever dying. All God wants is for her simply to resign herself to the fact that this man might never change. She is free to let go and leave him in the hands of God, just as I had to let go of my dream of seeing our church grow.

I had been brought to the brink of this resignation many times and had escaped each time "into the woods." I felt thankful for the friends who had helped me through difficult periods of shame during my sixteen years. I remembered different Bible characters in the story of Jesus' passion and crucifixion who drew a breath of silent courage and, while the crowds mocked, affirmed Him as loved, as special.

There was Mary, who had anointed His feet with tears and wiped them with her hair—so much like pastors' wives like Sally and Roberta who had ached and cried with me and prayed for a breakthrough. There was Simon of Cyrene, forced to carry Jesus' cross when he was an innocent bystander. How many, like my friend Mary, had stood by me, never expecting more from me than God was doing right now!

There was the centurion who, while others shamed Jesus, said aloud, "Surely this man was the Son of God." How I appreciated those who stuck by Bill and me—Beverly, Pam, the ministry leaders and others who saw something special about our church that was somehow obscured from the many. And I could hear the childlike exclamation of a woman in our church often rejected because she had been born "slower": "Melinda, no one ever loved me until I came to Church of the Risen Saviour."

Until Jesus' last moment, there were human beings who took their stand with Him, making feeble attempts to help Him through His pain. They were not the ones, except for Mary Magdalene, John and His own mother, that He might have expected. The thief on the cross, for example, had done little with his life until he mustered the courage with his final breaths to rebuke the other thief and stick up for Jesus. He thus affirmed Jesus as holy, and separated his own guilt from the sin-less character of Jesus Christ.

No wonder the Lord made sure these individuals received honorable mention when the Scriptures were written! No one knows how much it means until a friend, a co-worker or even a stranger risks his own honor to save yours.

But I also knew that I could never force anyone to that same place. I had no right to expect other women to let their dreams go. I could affirm them at the point of their shame and validate their pain because I knew how hard it was to die. To me their pain was holy, something I could not touch. I could only be a friend.

Besides, who was I to say which of their dreams had to die and which would be fulfilled? I could not destroy in someone else the hope on which faith is built, nor could I demand the spiritual mask of a smile in the midst of pain. I did not have to defend God or give up my expectations about anything else, only unite my will with His. Once it was dead, I could go on living knowing that God would somehow reward my willing-ness to trust Him.

When I woke up from my dream that night, I had seen beyond the crisis to the peace that could come afterward. But I needed help. There were still dregs of anger like a death shud-der trembling through a corpse. I sat at my desk that morning and wept. And the words came back: " . . . Who for the joy set before Him endured the cross, despising the shame, and has sat down at the right hand of the throne of God" (Hebrews 12:2). And, "He always lives to make intercession for them" (Hebrews 7:25). I needed His help and asked to be remem-bered in the throne room at that moment.

Then I remembered the words of a new friend I had found in another state only two weeks before. A woman named Sandy had spent years with an unanswered prayer—for a baby of her own. I recalled her words: "I woke up one morning realizing I was too old to give birth, that my dream was no longer possible. And I had to grieve its death." She grieved until anger gave way to resignation and then the pain left. God could say no to one prayer and yes to hundreds of others of lesser importance and she could be content.

So I let my dream die, and once it was dead I buried it, knowing that for a while there would be seasons of sorrow and tears, but a deep sense of peace that God had answered and said no. My shame was dead. I had no regrets, and knew I could finally be contented and happy without my dream. It was my highest act of worship. I had given God the thing I wanted most, and in giving it had touched the real God. When I touched Him and He took my dream away, I found out I loved Him more. And my hope in Christ—not in my dream—was still alive.

In order to be free to enjoy God, false hope must be amputated from true faith. Releasing the dream and letting it die is the only way to find out whether it was real or false. Sometimes it is not that the dream was false, but that it is not God's time for it to happen. This was the case with Abraham and Sarah, Zacharias and Elizabeth, Hannah and Elkanah. But letting go of it helps you to enjoy God now without having to struggle to hold onto something you cannot produce in your own strength.

After the dream dies, it is free to take another form. God is back in control rather than your own imagination, which has obscured God's real plan for your life.

I have let my dream go. I do not know if God will ever resurrect it, but now it is up to Him. Whether or not He does no longer has any bearing on my ability to serve Him joyfully today. And I will not entertain any thoughts of what might have been or may yet be. God's will is much better than my dream.

Once the dream is dead and you have gotten off the hope/disappointment roller coaster, you are ready to proceed with your healing to the next important phase—getting over any anger against God.

12

. . . .

Getting Over Anger with God

Answer yes or no to the following questions:

_____ 1. Am I reluctant to admit when I am angry?
_____ 2. Do I feel my temper flare but try to hide how I am feeling?
_____ 3. When I am angry, do I threaten to abandon others?
_____ 4. When I am angry, do I think of sabotaging myself with actions such as quitting or alienating others?
_____ 5. When reverses come, do I think God could have done something to stop it?
_____ 6. Do I blame God when things go wrong?
_____ 7. When I realize I am angry with God, do I refuse to pray?
_____ 8. Has my devotional life suffered recently?
_____ 9. When I read the promises of Scripture, do I think they apply to everyone but me?

_____ 10. Do I feel it was unfair for me to be born into the circumstances I was?

_____ 11. Does it seem that God blesses others but does not bless me?

_____ 12. Do I believe that God really cares about how I feel?

_____ 13. Does God seem emotionless?

_____ 14. Does God seem hard to communicate with?

_____ 15. Do I believe that if I am truly faithful, bad things are less likely to happen to me?

A person angry with God will probably answer yes to all but number 12. Answering yes to many of these questions indicates you are either angry with God now or will be soon.

Why Get Mad at God?

Anger with God has been going on since Satan fell from heaven. God, by His very position of authority, is subject to all sorts of criticism concerning the way He handles each situation in life. I wonder if Adam and Eve did not feel angry with God when they were driven from Eden. Since Adam did not really believe he was at fault and tried to blame his sin on the woman, I wonder if he grew angry thinking he did not deserve to suffer the consequences of sin by having to leave Eden.

Whether he did or not, the first biblical mention of anger at God is found in the book of Genesis with Cain, the son of Adam and Eve. Cain became angry with God when God did not regard his sacrifice of vegetables, though God *did* honor the animal sacrifice of his brother, Abel. The root of Cain's anger, then, was jealousy, which is usually at the root of anyone's anger with God.

Aren't we prone to wondering, when God crosses our will with His, why He could not do things our way? Any honest, thinking individual has probably questioned the Lord's wisdom at some point in his or her life. For many Christians, such questions do not usually arise over everyday matters, but over more serious matters, such as major loss and death. The next step is usually a flicker of anger that we squelch and let pass unnoticed as we attempt to defend God's position. We may rationalize away our anger so that we can continue to feel comfortable about trusting Him.

Throughout this book we have already met women who, when faced with the heartaches of living, found themselves questioning and even hating God for a season. The more intimate our relationship with any individual, the more comfortable we feel showing anger in his or her presence. And since God is committed to us eternally, we sometimes feel (even though we know it is probably irreverent) that He is responsible, at least indirectly, for the misery we suffer. After all, He could have prevented it and did not, right?

Complicating our dilemma is the belief that God allows reverses to come so that we can be tried in the furnace of affliction to prove whether or not our faith is real. A person already prone to anger with God may react, "Who does He think He is, anyway? What right does He have to make me suffer? Doesn't He already know what I'm really like? Can't He see into my soul?"

God does know each of us completely and is, as the Scripture says, "intimately acquainted with all my ways" (Psalm 139:3). He already knows all He ever needs to know about us. But what *we* often do not know is what our own reaction will be to having our will crossed by His.

To observe how anger with God develops, let's look at one woman's frustrating experience.

Lisa's Heart's Desire

Lisa grew up dreaming of the day she would marry and have children. Her longing to be a mother was more pronounced than that of her sisters. She always played with dolls and housekeeping toys. When she did not marry right out of high school, Lisa went reluctantly to college, where she met Harold.

Harold seemed to be the man she was waiting for. Handsome and kind, he showed interest in little children uncommon for young men his age. He had grown up in a large family, was used to looking after younger children, and he looked forward to a large family of his own.

Lisa and Harold, both Christians, were married shortly after college graduation. Eighteen months later the first of four children came along. Lisa lost herself in motherhood and family. She loved almost every aspect of housework and was skilled at sewing, baking, even canning. Her own needlework designs decorated the walls of their home.

Lisa and Harold attended church with their family every Sunday. She worked with the children; he sang in the choir after they attended prayer meeting each Wednesday night. It was in the choir that the trouble started.

One young woman, Dee, began to seek out Harold for advice in the wake of a ruined marriage. Each Wednesday night after prayer meeting and choir practice, Lisa noticed that Dee had something she needed to discuss with him. Then she began calling their home frequently asking if Harold could help her fix things around her house.

For a couple of months Lisa did not mind. She trusted her husband implicitly. Trying to put herself in Dee's position—a position she never wanted to be in!—she encouraged Harold to help her all he could. But Dee was attractive, if not almost sensuous in her appearance and manner.

One night after prayer meeting Lisa noticed that a strong attraction had developed between her husband and Dee. She tried to speak to Harold about it, but he sounded annoyed and accused Lisa of being ridiculous, so she tried to put her ever-increasing doubts aside. All the same, she was becoming resentful of Dee's requests for help from her husband. Why did she call only Harold and not some of the deacons for help? Also, the children kept asking where Daddy was.

Finally Lisa confronted Harold again. This time he blew up, accusing her of being a nag and not trusting him. Lisa realized she was lost in her world of homemaking and mothering, and tried again to rationalize away her feelings that this budding relationship was wrong. Perhaps, as Harold said, she was reading too much into it.

Almost frantically Lisa tried to put romance back into her marriage, but Harold was increasingly disinterested and even resentful of her efforts. He was no longer affectionate. Their sexual relationship became almost perfunctory. When Lisa made plans for them without consulting him, he was annoyed. She knew he was having to break promises to Dee.

Finally one morning Lisa's hopes were devastated when a woman in the church told her that Harold and Dee's relationship was the talk of the town. They had been seen together in a nearby city (by more than one person) having dinner together. When was Lisa going to wake up? This time when Lisa confronted Harold, she asked him to accompany her to marriage counseling. To her horror, Harold refused, and he went on to tell Lisa he was filing for divorce. He did not love her anymore and wanted out.

In one moment Lisa's lifetime dream was gone. All she had lived for was to be a good Christian wife and mother, to love and care for her husband and meet the needs of her family. And how was she rewarded for her noble goals? The same way other careless wives are rewarded for a more lackadaisical effort. How could this have happened? What had she done to deserve it?

Lisa almost fell apart mentally and emotionally. The only things holding her together were her children's need for emotional support and a few weakened shreds of faith in God.

She hired a good attorney who advised her to play the role of victim throughout the legal proceedings, which lasted several months. She did not have to act the part; she *was* a victim. Not only did Lisa feel victimized by Harold; she felt victimized by God. Why had He allowed this to happen? And at church? Wouldn't it have been better if they had never gone to church? Maybe they would still be married.

Lisa's heartaches were just beginning. In the coming months Harold's lawyer managed to reduce her child support to a minimal amount, increase Harold's visitation rights and make life miserable for her. She would have to go to work, give up the house and be content with financial survival whereas once they had lived comfortably. It seemed to Lisa that she was suffering for Harold's sins.

Harold married Dee within a month after the divorce was final, destroying Lisa's hopes for reconciliation. She still loved him and had been willing to forgive, but he had not given their marriage a second chance. After taking the best fifteen years of her life, he had left Lisa an emotional wreck, all but destitute financially and with her vision of a happy marriage destroyed.

Lisa got a job teaching at a Christian school and struggled, over the next ten years, to survive. She wanted to go on for a master's degree but, because she wanted to avoid public assistance, could not afford to go back to school and work, too.

The children, two boys and two girls, began to develop the roles children usually play in a dysfunctional home. The oldest, Steve, fourteen, became the hero, taking a part-time job to help his mother, whom he admired for her courage. He thought his father was a jerk and vowed never to be like him. He resented having to visit him and looked forward to the day he would not have to. His younger brother, Phil, was the mascot, breaking emotionally tense moments with laughter that was generally contagious, although Lisa knew he was suffering. He had never understood why his dad had just moved out one day when he was eight, and he secretly took some of the blame. The youngest child, Sophia, became the lost child, often shutting herself in her room to forget her pain. She felt distant from the other members of her family and had only one close friend.

But it was Linda, the next-to-the-youngest child, who began to give Lisa trouble. In order to numb the pain of her family's breakup, she began to run with kids from similar backgrounds. They drank and sometimes used cocaine. Linda did, too. More than once Lisa had to go down to the police station to spring her daughter from jail. Linda seemed to hate everything her mother stood for.

In spite of Lisa's efforts to hold her family together, she had failed. Not only had her marriage come apart, but her children were not eager to serve God. Linda had never given her life to Christ at all, and the others seemed uninterested in serving a God who had not been able to keep their home together.

Before We Shut Out Lisa

Lest you think Lisa's story rare, you should know that women like Lisa are not only members of our church and every church where I have spoken, but have been in every Christian audience I have ministered to in the past sixteen years. And they are increasing in numbers.

The no-fault divorce laws in this country have made it difficult for women like her. Where alimony is no longer legal, they are usually left destitute financially as well as devastated emotionally, often having to develop a new career to sustain themselves and their children, since their husbands hired a more skillful attorney or because the law does not favor women victimized in this manner. Nor does the women's movement champion their cause since it does not condone living out the role that they themselves have come to despise. To the women's movement, women like Lisa are examples of what devotion to a man will do for a woman. So Lisas fall between the cracks, unwanted even by women who understand what it means to be a victim of discrimination and abuse.

Unfortunately, in an effort to keep the standard of hearth and home alive for future generations, the Church often ignores situations like Lisa's. It is as though the Church, a large dysfunctional family with hurting members, is in denial about the existence of a disease of epidemic proportions. In our all-or-nothing approach to every issue, Christian teaching is usually geared to "normal" families. The problems Lisa faces are minimized or ignored.

Good Christian people who have been victimized by tragedies like hers are often passed over for leadership because their homes do not measure up. More than that, women in pain have nowhere to go to release their anger and find validation for their painful experiences, which would allow them to feel accepted by God and others just as they are. Being ignored in their hour of deepest sorrow only exaggerates the feeling of being abandoned by God. If He really cares, why don't His people care?

Unless something happens, we will become a nation and a Church full of emotional survivors, bitter and independent, fearing situations in which we must learn to trust.

How can a person in Lisa's position keep from being angry with God?

God and Prince Charming

Anger with God begins when a person has been victimized by pain and suffering. We know that this was not part of God's original plan, that this is God's "Plan B," but abstract theology does not touch us in our pain. In fact, theology—or our belief about who God really is—is part of the problem.

A distorted view of God is always a byproduct of pain and suffering. We perceive God based on our experience. The children of Israel, having been victimized by the Pharaoh of Egypt, had come to perceive themselves as victims in a land in which they had been reduced to slaves, their human dignity removed. As they fell under the taskmaster's whip, they felt forsaken by God.

Job encountered the same feeling when his grief and physical pain made him feel that God was not even aware of his suffering. King David, the man after God's own heart, felt abandoned by God at the moments when he suffered. The disciples after the crucifixion locked themselves away, hiding from the Roman government for fear they would be crucified, too. They felt disappointed and abandoned by the Master to whom they had given three years of their lives, forsaking everything to follow Him.

Lisa had led a sheltered life, growing up in a Christian home and church where stable families stayed together. She accepted Christ early and believed that if she followed the Lord, everything would work out fine. God would prevent her from making a mistake like marrying the wrong man or marrying a man who would leave her. She had prayed about marrying Harold and felt no resistance. Then, when Harold left, Lisa began to question God, since her view of Him had never included such a hitch as His unwillingness to make another human being follow Him.

But not only suffering produces a distorted view of God; so does prosperity. When we prosper, we tend to believe that God is on His throne and all is right with the world.

When we are in pain, on the other hand, and observe that the heathen are prospering, we envy them. Victims in a weakened condition hate the feeling of powerlessness that comes with being at the mercy of those who have control. Like a child fascinated with comic super-heroes in order to escape his own vulnerability, so the Church tends to look at God as the ultimate Super-Hero.

From childhood we are read stories of Prince Charmings who rescue Cinderellas and Snow Whites from wicked witches and stepmothers with a single kiss or a magical touch. We are read Scriptures about God's miraculous intervention in the lives of His people. Wounded women are fascinated with romance novels that paint a distorted picture of reality.

Television shows in which the hero "equalizes" the injustices inflicted by bullies on the defenseless are a commentary on the number of people who consider themselves victims. We can lose ourselves for a few hours in a world where wrong is avenged and people live happily ever after. Some ministers reinforce this distorted view of God by preaching about a God whose chief responsibility is to rescue each believer from every pain. Any pain experienced is always our fault, of course, because God is always good, and that means He always rescues.

But what happens when the rescue does not take place? Some people continue in denial. Others blame themselves. Still others fall away. But what they are falling away from is really a distorted view of God in which they have unwittingly placed their trust.

Lisa's trust was shaken because she had always felt that God would heed the cries of His children and rescue them from difficult situations. Lisa believed as a lot of Christians do that much of our suffering results from letting up in spiritual disciplines, like praying for loved ones. When Harold left suddenly, it was out of her hands before she had time to pray. This left Lisa feeling powerless. And like a child waiting for rescue from a super-hero, she could not believe that God would not move on Harold before the divorce was final.

He did not, and Lisa had nowhere to turn. She was ashamed before her Christian friends because they felt as she had—that failed marriages are the result of some omission on the part of the wife or husband. Now Lisa felt angry because her excellent Christian homemaking had not been rewarded with success. Her relationship with God began to falter because things were not working out at all as she had dreamed.

Finding the Real God

Lisa did not realize she had placed her hope in a distorted view of God and in a defective theology that left no room for the tainting brought about by a stubborn human being not open to God. In order for Lisa to recover faith, she would have to separate hope in the real God from hope in her fantasized perception of God. She would have to come to know the real God and decide if she would accept Him as He is. As with any relationship, the parties must discover the truth about one another and move from rude awakening to acceptance. Learning that God does not always rescue or provide escape from suffering was crucial to Lisa's recovery.

In the last chapter I shared how part of the process of letting my own dream die involved accepting God as Shadrach, Meshach and Abednego had, whether or not He rescued them from the fiery furnace. In one sense God did fail to rescue them, and they were thrown into the furnace. But the result of this "failure" provided the three men, and the king's court, with a revelation no one had ever seen—the appearance of the fourth Man like a Son of God in the furnace.

But even though this event turned out well and they were unhurt, God did not choose to rescue many others just as righteous as Shadrach, Meshach and Abednego. God did not rescue Abel, who had offered Him an acceptable sacrifice, from being killed by his brother Cain. God did not rescue the priests of Nob from being slain by King Saul. He did not rescue some of the early Christians from the hands of Saul of Tarsus or from the lions' jaws in the Colosseum at Rome. He did not rescue millions of Christians throughout the ages from sickness, poverty, disease and our last enemy, death. When He does not rescue us, He lets us see Him the way He really is, a God who moves according to grace, not works.

What God will finally rescue us from is hell. And whenever He does not choose to rescue us from our temporal pain and sorrow, He wants nothing more than our acceptance of Him. He dares to disclose Himself to us as the God who makes life-and-death decisions not on the basis of emotion, but of wisdom. And like any friend, what He wants from us is for our anger to give way to unconditional acceptance.

How Anger Touches God

The expression of anger is a form of self-disclosure in which we actually trust God with our most negative feelings about His will. I do not think God expects us to endure without anger. Anger is the emotion that releases our internal conflict in a form of expression that otherwise will consume us. The Bible exhorts us to lay aside anger (Ephesians 4:31), but first it must be recognized, acknowledged and expressed.

When Mary, the sister of Lazarus, reproved Jesus for not coming to her sick brother in time to heal him, He did not rebuke her. What she said was true. He does have the power to stop death. And He knows our frame; He remembers that we are but dust. He knows how deeply we are hurting because He has been here, too. So Jesus wept. He knew how Mary's hope in Him had been injured. And He had wanted desperately to stop Lazarus' death, too.

In Christ, God squeezed Himself into a human body so that He would become like one of us. The Creator wanted to feel what it was like to be the man, to experience every human emotion—joy, comfort, discomfort, pain—and to feel what it felt like to die.

During Jesus' passion, He learned what it felt like to want to live but to have to give up living. He found out what it felt like to be ashamed and misunderstood not only by unbelievers, but by friends like Mary, Peter and even John. He learned what it meant to be more alone than anyone has ever had to be. And He was completely and utterly abandoned by God so that we would never have to experience it.

The cross is an *I* with a subtraction mark through it: not my will, but Yours. The cross is the point in history where God's will was crossed with man's. Since that point was reached and God's anger was vented on Jesus, I am free to let go of my most heartfelt desires, even anger, because God let go of His. And the cross, the place where my will dies and unites with His, is the point from which I can move on in my relationship with Him.

Usually we do not really experience the cross on the day we first accept Jesus Christ as Lord and Savior. We experience it when we let go of our dreams, see them die and feel the release of our will into God's. When the independent will dies, anger with God usually shrivels up and dies soon after. That is why every one of us, I believe, must struggle as these wounded women have struggled through anger, hatred and pain to the place of death, so that we can experience resurrection. This may happen several times in our life as we undergo experiences that anger us and point up the glaring presence of our independent will. In each case we must acknowledge and express anger, and have it validated by others and resolved so that God can disclose Himself to us.

Recognizing when we have become angry with God—as Cain became angry before God warned him that "sin is crouching at the door" (Genesis 4:7)—can be the first step in finding out more about Him. Anger is not to be denied and avoided, but rather recognized, admitted and resolved. Until that happens, my independent will remains very much alive and working secretly against me. That is why it is so important for the Christian to be able to express his or her anger about God's will without feeling condemned. We need to allow ourselves and our Christian friends the freedom to show anger so that we can contact God at the point of honesty. To enshroud our anger in false yet spiritually correct responses serves to counterfeit brokenness rather than experience it.

Fortunately, Lisa's pastor recognized her deep sense of disillusionment with God. He helped her through her pain by allowing and even encouraging her to express her anger. One day in the hall at church he commented, "You know, Lisa, if that had been me, I think I would have felt very angry with God." For days Lisa couldn't get her pastor's comment out of her mind. How could a minister advocate expressing anger toward God? But a few days later Lisa was able to pull the plug on her stopped-up anger in the pastor's office and release a floodtide of bitter feelings. It was the first of several monthly sessions with her pastor, who continued to validate her pain and allow her to express emotion, however irreverent.

Thank heaven for such a pastor! He was aware that he, too, had been angry with God and knew that expressing it was the only way to freedom. I must say that I can hardly stand to be around Christians who are in denial about their own anger and deny others their right to express theirs. They usually effect soppy sweet countenances, fill their vocabularies with spiritual-sounding phrases and mask anger that comes out in more destructive forms. The Pharisees who preyed on Jesus were full of hidden anger covered with spiritually correct behavior. Jesus called them "whitewashed tombs which on the outside appear beautiful, but inside they are full of dead men's bones and all uncleanness" (Matthew 23:27). Some churches and Christian groups are full of people afraid to let down and be real. Not only the Lord but His sheep have been victimized by them.

It is nice to be in a church where it is O.K. to admit your

anger or that you have had a bad day. I like people who are not afraid to show they are normal and free from having to demonstrate "spirituality." Jesus came to make us more loving, not more "spiritual." I spoke recently at a church in our city. After the meeting one of my daughter's teenage friends ran up to me and exclaimed, "Oh, Mrs. Fish, I'm so glad I came. They told me I needed to hear you because you weren't spiritual. And you're not spiritual at all!" I knew what she meant—that I was not wearing a religious mask. It was the highest compliment she could have paid me.

Watch out for groups that are afraid to laugh at themselves. They are too concerned about being spiritually correct to be real. And since reality is the first step in self-disclosure, you will not experience much real intimacy in such an atmosphere. In fact, in those settings one usually encounters a Pharisaical resistance to self-disclosure. It is hard to put on a phylactery and take off a religious mask at the same time.

I used to hear Christians warn other Christians to watch their words—being careful, for example, not to mention particular illnesses, since "what you say is what you get." What a strain it was to keep from saying the word *flu*! I remember the day I gave up on it, thinking how freeing it would be simply to have a cold without figuring out what sin or slip of the tongue had made it fall on me. After Bill and I were freed from this form of religious bondage, a woman told me, "It's nice to have a pastor like Bill. When I heard him say that Sarah had diarrhea, I knew I could tell him that my daughter did, too."

When we are free from having to defend God, moreover, we can tell the truth without feeling we are betraying His reputation. His reputation needs no defense—unless, of course, we feel He is doing things that do not fit our mold, things we do not approve of.

Angry people are usually rigid, black and white in their doctrines, words and actions, afraid to let their real selves be seen for fear of being rejected by God. No wonder those in pain, like Lisa, are not accepted in many of our fellowships. Their spiritually incorrect experiences threaten our definition of what life ought to be or what God should be like. Why can't we let things just happen and let God defend or not defend Himself? Maybe we need to hear the Lord say, "Yea, verily, saith the Lord, get real!" And then we need to break down and really love people as they are, spiritually incorrect feelings and all.

But what if I'm not ready to die? Is it possible to get past the point of my anger and lack of understanding to restore communication with God?

Calling a Truce

When you are fighting an enemy nation and want to commence talks in the hope of restoring peaceful relations, those engaged in battle will call a truce. A truce does not mean we agree; it just means we have agreed to disagree and stop fighting about it. Perhaps at a later date during the truce we will see eye to eye, or at least be able to accept one another's position in the matter. Truces often lead to permanent peace.

You do not have to understand God's will or accept it unconditionally in order to call a truce. The truth is, God is not fighting but waiting until you stop fighting Him. As He told Saul of Tarsus on the road to Damascus, "It is hard for you to kick against the goads" (Acts 26:14). But when you stop fighting, the war will stop. Anyone who has ever fought with God has lost, including Jacob, who wrestled all night with the angel of the Lord and came away limping.

Nor will God be defeated or manipulated by passive-aggressive anger. He will allow you to take your toys and go home, but He will not give in once His mind is made up. Not talking to God is fruitless and ridiculous. Believe me, I know from experience.

When my father died of a heart attack at age 58 (as I have shared in my other books), I was devastated that he was not healed. In the beginning I looked for reasons to defend God's decision so that I could keep trusting Him, but eventually my emotions wore thin. I could find no reason. He had betrayed me, I thought. Why would He not heal? I had believed Him and never allowed a negative confession to escape my lips. But Pop had died anyway.

For months God and I were engaged in a test of wills. I was so angry with Him, so shattered in my confidence, that my faith was shaken to its core. I actually told God I hated Him, that I would not serve Him, that I would not even talk to Him. By not answering my prayer, He had, as far as I was concerned, made Himself my enemy. Fortunately, I have an understanding husband who allowed me to say bad things about God and simply hugged me and loved me anyway!

After six months or so I could take it no more. God was still blessing me in other areas. He was sickeningly nice to me, answering other prayers I had prayed that I considered less important than Pop's life. Besides, I didn't enjoy staying angry. Bill was in seminary. We were headed for the ministry! I had to get over this.

So I called a truce. I decided to bypass this issue for now and restore communication with God. There was no way I could bargain my father out of his grave.

"Lord, I don't understand why You took Pop," I said. "I would like to know. I had so many hopes and dreams. I don't know if I can ever fully trust You again to answer my heartfelt prayers. But I'll try. I'm willing to put this matter aside and go on to other things."

So I quit striking and went back to work. Sixteen years went by. During that time many wonderful things happened. Our children were born. The Lord gave us our ministry in Pittsburgh. I was preaching and teaching all over the area. I still did not understand why Pop had died, but somehow God made it O.K. In fact, I no longer even expected a reply.

One day I went to the doctor about a weight problem. He checked me thoroughly, took my blood and sent it to the lab. Because of my family history, he felt, I was a prime candidate for heart trouble. He recommended a lowfat diet and sent me home.

Leaping into the project with zeal, I bought a cookbook with heart-healthy recipes. And when I opened the book and started reading about diet and heart disease, I turned the page to a photograph of the plaque that had been removed from someone's artery. There it sat on a table like a plastic claw, hardened and ugly. My eyes filled with tears. This must be how Pop's arteries had looked.

In the gentlest voice, God whispered to me a private caption for the picture that only I could hear: *I didn't kill your father.*

In that moment, sixteen years after his death, I understood and let go of the last residue of anger. It was, if I may say it, like "forgiving" God. How could I have kept my father alive to face the agony of more years of irreversible heart disease? He was already suffering from another disfiguring disease. In a way, a heart attack had been a blessed, almost enviable way for him to die.

How glad I was that I had called the truce and not wasted sixteen years of fellowship with God! He always had my best interests at heart even when the evidence looked to me as though He did not. The Lord did not have to tell me why or help me to understand, but He had done even that. (And it wasn't the Bible He used; it was a cookbook!)

Giving God a Chance

Sometimes the problem is not that God will not do what we ask, but that it is not time for Him to act. All the pieces are not yet in place. As God told Abraham during a time when He was allowing their enemy's wickedness to run its course, "The iniquity of the Amorite is not yet complete" (Genesis 15:16). The Amorites were occupying the Promised Land during Abraham's life, but God was holding back judgment against them for a better time, the day of Joshua.

Patience is never acquired without tribulation. God is the ultimate in patience because He is the ultimate victim of tribulation. His original plan has been put on hold for thousands of years since the Fall of man and will be delayed until Christ returns! In order to be God's friend, it is necessary to accept this quality about Him. He is never in a hurry, yet He is never late. He has a perfect time for everything to come together. Sometimes He takes glory and pleasure out of using weakness to exaggerate the awareness of His might. But vindication from the Lord will come to everyone who waits on Him. And if you are going to wait on Him, let it be active rather than passive.

When you complain that the things the Lord has promised you have not come to pass, just remember, life isn't over yet. God has many creative ways of causing events to be woven together and bless our lives even if He will not answer our prayer right now. And won't we repent when He proves faithful after all, when His words to us are fulfilled and we did not give Him a chance?

This happened with Zacharias, the father of John the Baptist. The angel Gabriel announced John's birth while Zacharias was in the Temple. But Zacharias was so worn out on the hope/disappointment roller coaster, hoping for a son, that he refused to believe the Lord even when he saw an angelic visitation. This is real despair. But God had the last word, so to speak. Zacharias was struck dumb until the blessed event happened. Why? "Because you did not believe my words," the angel said, "which shall be fulfilled in their proper time" (Luke 1:20).

Jesus, too, came at the fullness of God's time when He was least expected. Recall the words of the Old Testament prophet: "The Lord, whom you seek, will suddenly come to His temple" (Malachi 3:1). And He did.

But expecting does not mean we have to ride the hope/disappointment roller coaster or become seasick watching each wave ebb and flow while we wait for the tide to come in. This only produces despair.

After Lisa's pastor allowed her to vent her anger, she found that God had a wonderful redemptive plan for her. She married a wonderful Christian man who appreciates everything about her that Harold threw aside. The children have gone through counseling and achieved a measure of healing. Even Linda has started attending church. Harold, meanwhile, is divorced from Dee. Lisa is glad she did not waste time hating God and staying bitter against Harold. And she is enjoying the fulfillment of everything she ever hoped.

What are you to do when you have experienced heartbreak, loss and disappointment? Busy yourself with enjoying the things God has planned for you *today*. Stay off the roller coaster by refusing to second-guess His timing. Once our will is subordinated to the Lord's, the dream can come to pass or not and we will not mind. We will not be so angry with Him that we do not enjoy the fulfillment of His promise when it does come.

If you are ready, let your dream die, and with it, anger with God that it has not happened. If you cannot let go of it yet, call a truce in your war against God. Let Him talk to you about what He wants to do right now, which may have nothing to do with the issue at hand. And if you cannot even do that yet, I understand. We can still be friends.

Now let's move on in our pathway to healing to the landmark of restoring fellowship with God. Do you wonder how to do that? The next chapter gives the secret.

13

● ●

Restoring Fellowship with God

Like the battle-scarred veterans of one of America's military conflicts, Christians often bear scars, too, token reminders of that less visible kind of conflict known as spiritual warfare. Jesus' resurrected body carries through eternity the prints of the nails and the wound of the spear in His side. They are the scars of His triumphant battle at the cross with the powers of darkness.

His scars are perhaps the only hint that will remind us in heaven of our earthly conflict between good and evil. But until the moment when every tear is wiped away by the loving hand of the Father, our souls and sometimes our bodies bear "the brand-marks of Jesus," as the apostle Paul called them (Galatians 6:17).

Jesus and Emotional Restoration

We learn from Jesus' example the extent to which emotional and spiritual restoration are needed after we have been wounded in battle. After He was tempted by the devil in the wilderness for forty days, the angels were sent to minister to Him. There were times when the pressure of ministry was so stressful that He called the disciples to a quiet place for much-needed rest. And after His resurrection Jesus returned to reestablish contact and to minister healing to His disciples.

Regardless of Jesus' prophecies of His own suffering and death, His followers had been caught emotionally unprepared. And afterward the ordeal of losing the One to whom they had committed themselves left them bruised. So for forty days Jesus walked among them to prepare them to live without His physical presence. He ministered to their emotional and spiritual needs in order to restore their souls. He even cooked dinner for them once by the shore of the Lake of Galilee. He was deeply interested in how they felt, and expressed forgiveness and understanding.

The wounded woman beleaguered by the stresses of the hope/disappointment roller coaster is in need of this same process of healing that Jesus initiated with His disciples.

Removing Shame

Since shame prevents self-disclosure and true intimacy, one of the main purposes of Jesus' visits with His closest disciples was to remove the shame over the way they had handled His suffering and death. Like Adam and Eve, whose shame over their sin caused them to hide from God, so the disciples, ashamed of their failure to stand with Him, hid.

Peter had already decided to return to his fishing nets and had launched out for a morning catch when the Lord interrupted him with the breakfast He had prepared on the shore. During that visit, the Lord called Peter back into the ministry, but first He called him back into fellowship. Three times Jesus opened up the subject of the bond of love between them:

"Simon, Peter, do you love me?" Only on the basis of his love for Jesus would Peter be able to feed the flock of God.

Feeling accepted rather than rejected by the Lord causes the wounded Christian woman to want to fellowship with God and serve Him. Feeling close to God again is the ultimate goal of the restoration process. It will involve (as we will discuss later in the chapter) stopping all forms of spiritual and emotional striving.

Having our sense of shame lifted by the Lord also causes us to want to lift the burden of shame from others. What we receive, we give. When others are free to disclose themselves and be accepted in our presence, our need to be perfect abates and we can be free, too. Giving acceptance and validation causes us to receive it.

One by one Jesus visited every disciple, restoring their souls after battle. During one of His visits Jesus breathed on each disciple in the Upper Room and said, "Receive the Holy Spirit" (John 20:22). As God the Father breathed into Adam the breath of life, so Jesus breathed into His new creations, those who had acknowledged His resurrection and Lordship, the restoring breath of spiritual life. This breath of God filled each one with a comforting presence of the Lord that, I believe, empowered them to wait for the outpouring of the Holy Spirit on the Day of Pentecost.

As Jesus had promised, He did not leave them comfortless. He came to them. Had their souls not been restored by His visit, it is likely that they would have been unable to wait for the power of the Holy Spirit (Acts 1:8) and would have abandoned the pursuit out of discouragement.

The wounded woman pursuing a fresh touch from God often feels undeserving of His love. Her anger at the abuses she has suffered on the hope/disappointment roller coaster, or her own low sense of self-esteem (fed by abuse at the hands of those who should have esteemed her), contribute to her inability to trust God to give of Himself freely. Many people who grew up in dysfunctional homes have difficulty asking God for their needs—even things He has promised every believer, like the Holy Spirit's power.

If you have a sense that you harbor a lack of trust, why not try asking the Lord to fill you with a renewed sense of His presence? Even if all others forsake you, the sense of God's abiding love will sustain you. Disclose your need to Him. He gives the Holy Spirit to those who ask Him. Jesus promised His disciples that God is not like a father who would give his son a stone in place of bread. God will fulfill the heart's desire of His child, especially when he asks Him for His presence. Why not ask right now?

Once we have been breathed on with God's breath, He gives us the courage to take the other necessary steps toward restoration. If the process of healing is to continue, the wounded Christian must cooperate with God in the next step.

Evacuation from the Battlefield

As the army evacuates its wounded from the battlefield, so the combat-weary soldier in the Lord's army needs to escape the line of fire in order to be restored. For a wounded woman, evacuating the battlefield will involve taking the steps necessary to remove herself from constant conflict. A battered woman needs to separate from her abusive husband until he has changed. Women in less life-threatening situations will feel as though they have indeed been evacuated from a battlefield as they set godly boundaries and refuse to respond to other forms of needless suffering and abuse. It may mean changing locations or simply finding an internal place of peace far away from the hope/disappointment roller coaster.

Whatever you do, make wise, calculated decisions, not impulsive, self-defeating ones. The wounded woman must thoroughly explore her options, as we discussed in chapter 5, for having her needs provided for before she makes a single move, unless her life is in danger. In those cases, immediate action is necessary, coupled with the resolve never to return. Many battered women go back to the abusive husband within days or hours after escaping. The abuse they suffer is invariably worse when they return because the husband punishes them for leaving.

Leaving the war zone is not only a natural principle but also a spiritual one. When Elijah defeated the prophets of Baal on Mount Carmel, he went away and hid himself in a cave to recover from the trauma of spiritual warfare and the depression that quickly ensued. As Jesus did with His disciples, Elijah took a personal retreat.

A young mother may have responsibilities she cannot shirk, but relief from the stress of unnecessary activities may be crucial to her healing. Some women have become so involved in church and school activities that their self-worth hinges on participation in them. This defines a sick, codependent involvement.

Temporary withdrawal from these activities will give you time to heal and others a chance to learn to live without your rescuing efforts. As you heal, the Lord may either put you back into those activities or change your direction completely, pruning back the vines for more abundant fruit production in ways you never knew about while you were caught up in the cycle of codependency. But when you institute change . . .

Be Prepared for Disapproval

The next time you go crabbing, remember it is perfectly safe to place all your crabs in a bucket without a lid. Each time one crab tries to crawl out, the others will drag him back in. If only they would cooperate to reinforce and encourage each other, they could all escape, but they don't. So it is with anyone who breaks the denial surrounding her presently dysfunctional situation at home or elsewhere and breaks free of the control of others. Those in bondage who are afraid of change and unwilling to break denial will resist and try to pull you back in—using guilt projection, threats and manipulation, if necessary—to preserve the status quo.

Be warned that some people, even those close to you who do not understand, may be angry with you for retreating from the battlefront. But when you are wounded, retreating from the battle in no way makes you a traitor. In order to get back into the battle at a later date, you must take care of yourself now. You are no good to yourself, your family, your job or your church in an emotionally devastated condition. You cannot enjoy God or His blessings each day when you are dodging the arrows of spiritual, emotional and physical warfare.

A Healing Separation

Clint and Marcie sought out Bill and me for marriage counseling when separation divided their fourteen-year marriage. Before leaving her husband, Marcie had been devastated on the hope/disappointment roller coaster with her compulsive-addictive husband and had wound up in a state of emotional despair. Her countenance bore the emotionless stoicism common to many wives victimized by their husbands' continued misdeeds over a period of years.

Clint was a drug addict who had come to the Lord and left drugs, but had never opened up his gambling addiction to the Lord's healing. Counseling sessions revealed that Clint not only gambled but drank (despite his former drug addiction) and manifested symptoms of sexual addiction. While Marcie worked hard as a computer technician, Clint spent her earnings frivolously. Marcie's faithfulness stood out against Clint's compulsive job-changing.

Clint was also a religious addict, having jumped from one healing ministry to another, sometimes leaving his wife and three children five or six nights a week to attend services where he felt he could see God's power demonstrated. He had given large amounts of money to ministries that did not sow much back into his life. He had become compulsively involved in at least seven different ministries over a ten-year period.

Clint was in denial about how much Marcie had been affected by his compulsive-addictive behavior. She was weary of trying to get through to him and felt hopeless that Clint would change.

He would admit, for his part, that he had done things he was not proud of, but his denial had never been broken through. Still thinking the bulk of their problem lay with his wife's leaving, he continued to quote Scripture to Marcie about her obligations as a wife to forgive him and move back home.

Clint had brought his wife to us expecting us to affirm his position, and was amazed to find that we did not advise immediate, unconditional reconciliation. Marcie needed to get off the hope/disappointment roller coaster. Clint needed the separation to help break denial about how badly he had hurt his wife and family with his addictions, and to prove to her that he was willing to change by seeking and receiving professional counseling. He seemed as irritated with Bill and me as he had apparently been with at least five counselors before us who refused to stand with him "for his marriage," as he put it. Covering his unwillingness to look deeply at the wounds he had caused, Clint kept shoving Marcie further away, all the while quoting Scripture to her.

Clint gave the impression that Marcie was keeping God's will on hold by her unwillingness to forgive, forget and move back in. He was projecting guilt onto her for moving out, rather than seeing that the root of the problem was his own sick behavior. As he spun out of control through the addictive cycle, she traversed the peaks and valleys of hope, crisis and disappointment until she could no longer feel anything for the husband she had once loved.

Gently we explained to Clint that his job was to cause Marcie to want to move back in. He needed to win her love and trust all over again if the marriage were to be restored. If he did not, no amount of external pressure from counselors or pastors would cause Marcie to enjoy being married to him. The emotional damage he had caused was something only he and God could repair—if Clint would cooperate with God. We would not resort to using shame, the lowest form of motivation, to pressure Marcie back to Clint's house, a place she did not want to go.

Evacuating the battlefront is the first step toward the soul's restoration. Whether it is a geographical or emotional separation or both, "God has called us to peace" (1 Corinthians 7:15). In that season of peace, wounds are given a chance to close and the healing process is begun.

Evacuate anyplace where your conscience bothers you. God wants your conscience healed so that you can surrender to Him, not to the devil's wiles substituting for your conscience (perhaps through false guilt projected onto you by people who disagree with what you are doing). Women who have been abused spiritually and emotionally are afraid to go back to the Lord and sometimes back to church. The condemnation they expect to receive for having "failed" is too great a barrier to overcome when they are in a fragile emotional state.

Naomi left Moab because, in her fragile emotional state of suffering, she felt God did not want her there. Searching for restoration, she summoned her courage and last bit of energy to get back to Bethlehem in time for the barley harvest. And while she felt angry and abandoned by God, her conscience led her back to the place where she felt she could receive either God's rebuke or His healing. She received His restoration, of course.

Maybe it is time for you to go home—not to pain this time, but to the Lord.

Restored to Fruitfulness

Evacuating the battlefront and reattaching the severed cord of fellowship with God are important to being nurtured by God back to a place of health where you can once again bear fruit. But God's interest in your healing is not motivated chiefly by His "need" for you to be fruitful. Too many women view their recovery in terms of their ability to help others, as though they are unworthy to be healed or restored unless God uses it at some later date to help others. While helping others later may be a byproduct of your restoration, restoring your life is more important to God than your ability to produce.

This is a secret Leah never learned. The first wife given to Jacob always sought to win Jacob's love through childbearing. And while she bore him ten sons, it was Rachel he loved. God's love for you is already assured and constant. It is based not on performance or production but on who you are.

Rest

The first four letters of the word restoration spell *rest*, which is where restoration begins. Without rest from battle, wounds cannot heal and the soul cannot be restored. It is much easier, once the sounds of war are fading in the distance, to hear what God has to say to you. But the wounded woman herself has to choose rest. She must see it as motivated not selfishly but spiritually.

The place of rest is the place God calls every believer before he or she does a single work for God. A lesson for the overworked Christian is found in Leviticus in the consecration ceremony for the priesthood. Each priest—after being called out of the camp, cleansed, clothed with his priestly garments and anointed with the blood of the sacrifice of ordination and the holy anointing oil—reached a point when the ordination ceremony had to stop. During a break the new priest did nothing but sit in the Holy Place of the Tabernacle for seven days. He had to learn to rest before he served, to sit in God's presence before he offered a single sacrifice.

The heavenly Father, according to Jesus, seeks worshipers, not workers (John 4:21-24). Before God calls us to fruitfulness, He wants us to stop striving and know that He is God (Psalm 46:10). It is performance-oriented emotional and spiritual striving that have led the wounded woman on the hope/disappointment roller coaster in the first place. Sometimes even the spiritual disciplines of prayer and Bible reading, when they become obsessive, can interfere with restoration.

Stop Fruitless Praying

One way to stop striving is to stop forms of fruitless praying that wear the believer out. Prayer is simply talking to God and listening to Him. When a Christian woman engages in long-term, intense intercession coupled with emotional longing for a situation that is not to be, she risks boarding the hope/disappointment roller coaster, hoping her heartfelt desire will be rewarded. The stronger-willed she is, the longer she will ride the roller coaster, never seeing her prayers answered.

It was such intense praying that led Lynn, whom we met in chapter 2, to gradually lose faith in God while praying for more than 25 years for her husband to be saved. It was difficult for

Lynn to sit by while God was saving other women's husbands, so Lynn began to "work."

Sometimes sermons or teachings we hear at church on topics like intercession throw well-meaning Christians into spiritual panic. Wanting to make sure they are doing everything they can to ensure that their earnest desires come to pass, they throw themselves headlong into obsessive praying. This form of praying counterfeits intercessory prayer, which may generate intense feeling but is motivated (unlike obsessive praying) by God. When praying is motivated by God, there is an ease with which the one praying feels that he or she is being carried through.

The woman engaged in obsessive praying, on the other hand, fixates on a particular conclusion and submerges all her emotional faculties into praying or "believing" for it. She may even concoct visions and auditory hallucinations that seem to her, during the course of her obsession, like the voice of God and corroborate her belief that her intercessory experience is real. Deep down, though, she has the feeling she is initiating the intensity rather than being carried in a flow. When the prayer is not answered and she cannot keep up her intensity for weariness, she may feel fear that her prayer will not be answered and anger at being rebuffed by God in her hour of sorrow.

Obsessive praying, instead of accomplishing much (James 5:16), has the power to destroy a woman's sense of closeness to God as she rides up and down on the hope/disappointment roller coaster toward despair.

What propels this devotion is usually human-initiated rather than God-initiated desire. Sometimes in the beginning it is not easy to tell the difference. When answers to prayers are not forthcoming, however, it is good to recognize that you are not in the flow of God's stream and stop. This is much closer to being led by the Spirit than engaging yourself in fruitless praying, the end of which is despair.

Sometimes the obsessive pray-er feels that to let go is to allow the devil to get the upper hand and win the warfare. What we need to see is the finished victory of Calvary that allows us to be still and watch the Lord work for us. Should the time come for increased fervency, and if it is God's will for us to keep praying, He will give us help, as He did Moses whose arms were lifted by Aaron and Hur to keep the vigil going.

Above all, the believer should never allow herself to be pushed out of a sense of rest in God. When the activities of praying, fasting, giving and serving become driven, she has passed from rest into works. A woman in the works mode resents others who are not suffering with her.

A Sufferer's Resentment

Sometimes a wounded woman feels she is being forced to suffer while others are not, especially when she is sincerely doing all she knows to do. At this point she becomes overwhelmed by a need to justify her suffering, which is sometimes self-induced or self-magnified. Unfortunately, this self-justification rails against others who are not suffering or not striving for answered prayer and fruitfulness in the same way she is. The woman "working" for her salvation or spiritual fruitfulness feels as a missionary to a third-world country does when he comes home on furlough, or a war veteran feels when he returns home to see America involved in business as usual while his limbs are torn off and his buddies are dying. Resentment over the seeming prosperity of others is a form of reverse culture or reentry shock faced by wounded women, too.

As striving increases, resentment increases, putting the wounded woman on a treadmill of bitterness and unforgiveness. Not far behind is a sick desire to see others suffer, too. If others are not suffering with you, it is tempting to project guilt onto them for not suffering. The idea that only those who are spiritual suffer, in preparation for being used mightily, makes the proud feel more proud and those at rest feel guilty—unless they see behind the guilt projection.

The newsletter of one minister that we receive regularly points up his own suffering cast against a backdrop of others in the Body of Christ who do not seem to be going through the same intense trials. His preoccupation and lack of emotional healing and restoration have set him up for a subtle form of pride. Thinking that his part in the divine plan is more crucial than that of others, he perceives that he has been singled out for more intense forms of spiritual attack. He has also developed a fear that the devil's attacks will only increase in magnitude, that God is somehow permitting this, and that if others were truly devoted to the Lord, they would be suffering, too.

He has fallen prey to the victimization deception and is one step from paranoia that pushes him off a place of rest. The best thing he can do for his ministry is to cease striving, get into emotional recovery—something he repudiates—and stop victimizing the Body of Christ, trying to make them feel guilty about being at rest in the Lord. His emotional wounds have seduced him out of rest and into a subtle bondage to works.

Being Reattached to Others

Women recovering from domestic battle wounds or from grief desperately need a safe place for self-disclosure—in effect, a "troop ship" experience (much as war veterans returning from battle share their trials and triumphs on the decks of troop ships) in which they can relive their experiences with their peers who have suffered similar loss. One reason for the development of resentment is the feeling of isolation that drives many who are suffering pain to hide. The sense of shame combined with depression causes many women separated from their battleground to feel lonely and afraid.

The problem is magnified when their form of suffering has involved relationship addiction. Many women have suffered not one abusive relationship but several. The wounded woman who has been victimized by controlling men finds it as difficult to stay away as if he were an addictive narcotic. Unless she has a well-established support system, false guilt lures her back to the place of victimization.

Reliving the troop ship experience reattaches her to the Lord's presence in others. Notice that Jesus appeared to His disciples more often after the resurrection when they were meeting together. He commits Himself to group healing. If a woman has been battered, the batterer's jealousy has made him seek, through threats and manipulation, to isolate her from her relatives and closest relationships. The shame of having your relatives and friends insulted by your batterer may prompt you to separate from them, but reattaching yourself to these or other healthy relationships is vital.

Let me suggest three ways you reattach yourself to others.

The Troop Ship Experience

The first way is the troop ship experience in which you meet with other women in recovery from your particular form of grief. Women recovering from the pain inflicted by abusive men need other women to hear them out and let them know they are accepted. The recognition of mutual experience causes a bond to develop. Hearing the stories of their experiences will help you see how you have been victimized not only by the misogynistic behavior of the abuser, but by a pattern of behavior in yourself.

Women going through divorce, parents who have lost children, and widows can also profit from such a group. To know that your experience is common and that you are not the one who is crazy will restore the sense of self-confidence it takes to live alone. Women who find themselves alone for the first time in many years, particularly if they are infected with codependency, sometimes have panic attacks—the onslaught of sudden fear—in places like shopping malls. Hearing from others undergoing the same experience helps you see it as an understandable reaction to your stress.

Call a women's shelter or hotline that has information about support groups in your area to see if a women's codependency support group is meeting. If you are escaping physically or emotionally from an alcoholic, try Al-Anon, the worldwide organization for those who live with alcoholics. If you have been battered, it is essential to escape and learn to live without the addictive power of the hope/disappointment roller coaster.

One word of caution. Sometimes women in recovery slip into attitudes that contribute to the development of man-hatred. Move through this attitude to a place of healing. Recognize your hatred of men and make it a matter for prayer and, if necessary, professional counseling. When discussions roll around to man-hatred, it is good for someone in the group to point out that attitude. It is likely that for the number of abusers you can think of, there are as many or more good men standing quietly in the background of your life—uncles, brothers, brothers in Christ whose presence you have ignored while you have focused your attention on the mean ones. All men are not misogynists; in fact, the majority are not.

A Healthy Local Church

A second kind of reattachment is found in a healthy local church. I say *healthy* because not all church atmospheres, unfortunately, are conducive to recovery. Check your church first to see if there are women in recovery there. If not, you might start a group with your pastor's permission. While you have been lost in your pain, you may be unaware that the wider Church has been moving into ministries of recovery.

We are all waking up to realize that the Lord is doing a new thing in the earth. I believe He is preparing the Church for a great harvest into His Kingdom, but this time He wants the Church to be ready. The ingathering will include addicts, men and women from dysfunctional homes and those who have been wounded emotionally. Enjoying God and His blessings will hinge on whether or not these broken hearts are healed. God is preparing new wineskins for the new wine. Many churches are changing their formerly legalistic attitudes concerning psychology, counseling and support groups. Ask about your own church's attitude toward recovery.

Find a local church supportive of the steps you have taken to remove yourself from the battlefield. It would be difficult to recover if every Sunday you had to hear denunciations of counseling, support groups or inner healing from the pulpit. It is likely that churches that denounce these things are themselves full of non-recovering addicts, adults who grew up in dysfunctional homes and wounded people who are deeply angry and rigid in their attitudes. Angry denunciations are an evidence of frustration in a minister. Talk to him respectfully about your concerns without judging him.

My husband and I labored for years under the delusion that quick-fix solutions like more prayer, more miracles or more Bible reading would solve these problems. I thank God for those who prayed for us to see the light. Our church moved into recovery together because Bill and I as the pastors saw the need for it. What an eye-opener to discover that fully ninety percent of our members were adult children of alcoholics! My heart goes out to pastors struggling with problems that will never go away without process rather than quick-fix solutions.

Advocating only a quick-fix approach in these circumstances (which is not to bar a miracle!) is the pathway to sure ministerial burnout.

Be patient but do not sacrifice your own recovery while you wait for the minister to get the revelation about recovery.

Churches in which women are put down or where their leadership is unwelcome are not, in my opinion, healthy places for women in recovery. This attitude is a sign of rigidity that will be evident in the church's approach to every issue. Find a church where the "lid is off" women as well as men, where everyone is free to "glorify God and enjoy Him forever."

The addictive church is one that exists to perpetuate itself rather than facilitate others' knowledge and enjoyment of God. Becoming part of someone else's empire-building will suck you into a codependent involvement with a church that is, without realizing it, spiritually abusive. This can happen in a denominational or non-denominational setting.

Look for a healthy pastor, an emphasis on love and grace, equal opportunities for women and men, and the absence of that sense of being driven to serve God in order to please Him. Ask yourself: Do people really enjoy themselves here? Will they accept and love me as I am? Do not let your dysfunctional issues separate you from your brothers and sisters in Christ and deceive you into thinking that God's children do not care. I, for one, do care, and there are many more like me in the Church!

Healthy Friends and Relatives

The third suggestion is detaching yourself for now from friends and relatives who are unhealthy, and reattaching yourself to healthy friends and relatives who will support your recovery. Relationships can facilitate or destroy recovery. Someone who encourages you to look for what would amount to a new codependent relationship to replace an old one is not giving sound advice. You need to learn what drives you toward unhealthy relationships so that you do not get sucked in again.

Avoid people who drain you, taking and giving nothing in return. Some relationships need to be put outside your borders for you to enjoy peace in your land. You may find that you must make a whole new set of friends. Healthy relationships are those that promote your relationship to Jesus Christ and offer emotional support, while unhealthy ones seek to separate you from Jesus Christ and wear you down emotionally. Think about it. Ease yourself out of commitments to and situations with people who are unhealthy or not recovering. Surround yourself with people with whom you can be real and accepted.

Real Faith

Since Jesus Christ's strength is perfected in weakness, it is all right for us to show our weakness, even if it means disclosing a lack of faith. Human-initiated faith must be fueled with fleshly effort, while rest comes to the believer who has been given real faith for Christian living. God-initiated faith causes a Christian to be at rest and yet not apathetic in his desire to see prayers answered. God-initiated faith is devoid of anxiety. Often the anxiety comes when we need to prove something about our faith in order to remove our sense of shame at not seeing our heart's desires come to pass. False faith is the enemy of restoration because it creates anxiety and a sense of hopelessness.

Paul wrote about a faith that is at rest when we die to our dream, when our will is united with Christ's: "If we died [together] with Him, we shall also live with Him; if we endure, we shall also reign with Him; if we deny Him, He also will deny us; if we are faithless, He remains faithful. . . ." Why? "For He cannot deny Himself" (2 Timothy 2:11-13). Once we know that our place in God's heart is secure, our human faith may waver with circumstances, but we know God will keep us.

We experience real faith, real intercession and real hearing from God when we stop our striving and show our weakness. "Blessed are the gentle, for they shall inherit the earth. Blessed are those who hunger and thirst for righteousness, for they shall be satisfied" (Matthew 5:5-6). Each of the Beatitudes identifies some form of weakness or inferiority in the world's eyes as the key to God's power. Until we get the message and disclose our own weakness, we tie God's hands. What if God blessed striving? We would be forever caught in a web of works!

Real vision and prayers have a resurrection life of their own that we will never discover until we stop trying to defibrillate them with human effort. If you feel you are the one controlling the prayer, fasting or other effort to "touch" God, perhaps it is time to get off the roller coaster of fruitless praying and stop. Then wait for God to plant His aspirations in you. When He does, it will be easy and fruitful to ask, seek, knock. While praying may occasionally be intense, you will have the sense not of a salmon swimming upstream but of being carried in God's flow.

Real Prayer

Listening to God, rather than badgering Him with requests that are not His intent to answer now, will reopen the channel of communication with God. Let God change the subject. Perhaps He wants to minister to another area of your life first with His healing touch. Maybe the answer to your prayer will not come for ten more years. In the meantime, give God your ear.

Make yourself still, cease effort and wait for God to initiate spiritual activity or desires in you. This is submission. If after a while you do not sense that your efforts are fruitless in His eyes, go ahead and make plans, but always hold them loosely so that He may change your course.

It is necessary not only for the wounded woman to stop fruitless praying in order to keep her sense of closeness to God, but to be able to receive comfort and healing from the words of Scripture.

But that is not always easy.

Is There Help in the Bible for Wounded Women?

When Marcie began her recovery after she moved out on her compulsive-addictive husband, she realized that for a long time she had had difficulty reading the Bible and praying. Having been brought up on the Scriptures, Marcie had difficulty reading any passage of Scripture without feeling guilt. It was as though every passage set off the voices of ministers she had heard over the years whose admonitions had not always been affirming or insightful. She could also hear her husband's voice superimposed over the words of Scripture, chiding and rebuking her.

Practically every passage in the Bible had been pigeonholed over the years into categories of principle and doctrine. It had come to be simply a list of *thou shalts* and *thou shalt nots*. Some passages had been invoked so rigidly—particularly ones about women, marriage and divorce—that whenever she heard them, she was blocked from any insight by painful emotional associations. So Marcie found herself avoiding Bible reading. She got more out of reading secular psychology books that validated her experiences and did not condemn her for her pain and frustration.

This unfortunate phenomenon has afflicted nearly every Christian I know in recovery, men and women who have entered emotional recovery from addictions, compulsions, abuse and codependency. It is as though the words they once turned to for the answers to life have disappointed them. God let them down, and His Word is no longer helpful or cannot be trusted. What went wrong?

The rigid Christian would immediately conclude that this is prime evidence that the recovery movement is of the world, the flesh or the devil because it seeks to sever the believer from the Word of God as its basis for authority. But this is not true. A deeper look into these lives will reveal people who really love God, who want to understand God's ways and who have a respect for Scripture as the infallible Word of God, even though they seem to avoid it.

Their experience is similar to that of the Jews with the Law when Jesus came on the scene. The scribes and Pharisees had so categorized and enshrouded it with their traditions that finding God through the Scriptures was difficult.

When Jesus came out of the wilderness, on the other hand, He instituted a new way to teach. Although He began His ministry in His hometown synagogue reading from the Scriptures, His hearers did not like His interpretation. After reading from the prophet Isaiah about the mission of the Messiah, He told them, "Today this Scripture has been fulfilled in your hearing" (Luke 4:21). They were enraged. Later He told the Pharisees, "You search the Scriptures, because you think that in them you have eternal life; and it is these that bear witness of Me" (John 5:39).

Reading the Bible alone up until that point had not delivered anyone. They still needed a living Messiah, the embodiment and fulfillment of the Scriptures. Tragically, most of the Jews who were most devoted to Bible reading missed their day of visitation because Jesus did not fit their scripturally well-defined doctrines and traditions.

I wonder if that is why Jesus hardly ever preached from the Bible. Except for the words He spoke to the disciples on the Emmaus road and occasional references to prophecies about the coming Messiah—and usually these were added by the New

Testament writers—Jesus broke tradition and preached about the glory of His Father's relationship to men and women, told heartwarming stories about fathers and children, recounted tales of soldiers or farmers, used the images of an agrarian society. All this served to *conceal* spiritual truth from the Bible-believing Pharisees and *reveal* it to honest, God-fearing folks who had not gotten much understanding about God from the letter of the Law.

These same people devoured the spirit of the Law. Jesus synthesized the Law and the prophets, reducing the piles of scrolls carried around by the Pharisees and scribes to two commandments: Love God with all your heart and being and love your neighbor as yourself.

When our love of the Bible short-circuits our love of God and people, haven't we missed it?

I think you can tell from the illustrations in this book that I love the Bible and see recovery and healing in its pages. Recovery is nothing more than the grace that is in Christ Jesus synthesized into an easily understood form. And to tell you the truth, some of the psychology books I have read recently have opened my eyes to see more of God's mercy in His Word than dozens of sermons from a legalistic point of view.

The problem is not with the Book but with the reader who has an eye full of the darkness of legalism (see Matthew 6:22-23). Rigidity is one of the emotional elements present in dysfunctional family tradition. It governs the victim's approach to life, including his approach to the Bible. But when the doctrines formed out of legalism and tradition drop off like scales, you will find the dimension that Adam and Eve lost at the Fall—the ability to see ourselves, others and God with the dimension of grace. Until then the Bible never affords comfort, only legalistic injunction.

A Fresh Look at the Word of God

So before you throw the Bible away and disregard it as not needed in recovery, try taking a fresh look at it. The day that Saul of Tarsus came to the crossroads of his life on the Damascus road, God removed his eyesight for three days. Blinded by the vision and hearing the Lord identify Himself as Jesus, the very One he had been persecuting, was too much for Saul to bear. He sat for three days neither eating nor drinking, wondering, I am sure, if he would ever see again. As the legalist, after all, he probably thought he deserved to be punished permanently for murdering the servants of the Lord.

But after three days a Christian named Ananias, sent to him by means of a vision from God, came into the room where Saul sat, laid hands on him and prophesied. "And immediately there fell from his eyes something like scales . . . " (Acts 9:18).

When the scales fell from the eyes of this self-labeled Pharisee of the Pharisees, God changed his entire perspective on Scripture. Instead of throwing it aside, Paul spent thirteen years before he began his ministry immersed in it, reveling in the revelation of the grace of God that his Pharisaical legalism had obscured. Now he knew not only the letter of it, but the Spirit behind it and the Christ in it.

Paul wrote later to Timothy that "the goal of our instruction is love from a pure heart . . . " (1 Timothy 1:5). And this former Pharisee wrote 1 Corinthians 13, and also wrote, "Put on love, which is the perfect bond of unity" (Colossians 3:14). Every letter Paul wrote referred to grace as though it had been to him the most breathtaking revelation. He could not get enough of it, spending the rest of his life growing in the love of God and of the brethren and the glory of His grace.

So it is possible for the scales to fall away. What can I do to restore my faith in the Scriptures?

Why not start by obtaining a new version of the Bible? Not long ago I happened to pick up an old Bible I had used during my worst period of emotional pain more than twenty years ago. Immediately a feeling of sadness penetrated my soul. It was not the Bible itself, I realized, but the mental associations I had made with that particular copy of the Bible. Buying a new Bible in a translation you can understand can break a painful emotional barrier that may be hindering you.

Next, begin your study by taking a fresh look at all the old passages once overlaid with a dark film of legalism. Before you read, ask God to let the eyes of your heart be enlightened by the Holy Spirit so that you can see the Lord's love and grace toward yourself and others. Read the Scriptures with the understanding you have gleaned about human nature from personal observation and through studying other sources.

When I began to understand the principles of the dysfunctional home, and God began to open my eyes to a deeper understanding of grace through my own recovery, the Bible became a new book. I quickly learned to see its characters through new eyes, as struggling with low self-esteem, isolation, denial, perfectionism, rigidity and codependency. The terms are not in Scripture but the experiences are, because they are common to man. Now I enjoy preaching grace and seeing His mercy in the life of every character in the Bible, even characters out of Leviticus!

Take a fresh look at Jesus' life and ministry and that of the early Church. Where there appear to be discrepancies, study them out to find the thread of consistency in the words of Paul and Peter that affirm rather than negate the grace approach to everything—even the book of Revelation and the Last Judgment! You will have to look deeper than the surface, but you will not have to twist the Scriptures to make them fit your mold.

When your tightly held doctrines choke out grace instead of extend it, call those doctrines into question and readjust your traditions to conform not to the "oldness of the letter," but the newness of the Holy Spirit. Avoid speculations and flaky interpretations. Check things out with people whose lives with God mirror His grace and mercy in a mature way. Talk questions over with your pastor.

The purpose of emotional healing is to restore you to a sense of closeness with God. Reattaching the severed cord of fellowship gives you the ability to abide in Him and bring forth fruit. Now let's look at what kind of fruit He is looking for and where it is nurtured.

14

• • • • • • • • • • • • • • • • •

Taking Your Place

As the wounded woman recovers from the barrenness syndrome and moves into emotional health, she begins to recover her fellowship with God, which automatically means she will begin to bear fruit, both natural and spiritual, seen and unseen. In the natural realm (traversing the range from seen to unseen), you may bear fruit ranging from children to increased job productivity to simply a greater enjoyment of life. In the spiritual realm, you may see more friends come to Christ, more fruit of the Holy Spirit, more spiritual gifts released in your life.

As a woman is restored to health and matures spiritually, her capacity to love will be enlarged, while properly set boundaries will preserve her fruit from the destructive power of the enemy. Universally applicable boundaries for women are found in three areas of influence: her home, her children and her church. Let's look at each of these and how false boundaries within them may quench the Holy Spirit and squelch a woman's natural expression.

A Woman's Place at Home

A woman's place, the saying goes, is in the home; and few would argue that fruit-bearing for anyone, man or woman, begins right there. When Paul wrote his directions concerning leadership for the newly formed churches, he always saw the Christian's behavior in the home as the litmus test for real spiritual fruit.

But what *is* a woman's place in the home?

For the single woman, this is no issue. She is the only one at home and is, therefore, the undisputed head of it. She sets her own limits and determines how she will spend her time, making decisions that govern her life with the Lord as her guide. Whether she seeks the input of pastor, counselor or friends is (unless her decisions conflict with the rights of others) entirely up to her. Paul exhorted singles to undistracted devotion to the Lord, and he affirmed singleness as the lifestyle he preferred.

Scripture exhorts the married woman to glorify God in a different way. Any group, naturally, needs government. Decisions must be made that govern all the members of the group and determine how time, energy and money should be expended. When a Christian woman chooses to marry, she chooses a life that gives her husband the responsibility (more than just the right) to make the final decision. "The husband is the head of the wife, as Christ also is the head of the church" (Ephesians 5:23). As I have mentioned earlier, the word *kephale*, translated "head," actually means originator or source rather than authority. A woman is asked by the Lord, moreover, to submit only to her husband, not to another's husband or to men in general.

Marriage was created to establish a home environment in which nurturing could take place, children could be brought forth and everyone could follow the Lord. Once Satan entered the picture, however, all this changed. People do not naturally flow together in perfect agreement one hundred percent of the time. Nor is the husband always right, nor does he have the Lord's opinion in every matter. No husband in his right mind would claim such infallibility! What God *is* saying is that mutual submission in the fear of Christ is His first order; and when a conflict of opinion arises in the home and creates an impasse, let the wife defer to her husband so that a stalemate may be alleviated.

If he is wrong, God will allow him (as we have already seen) to run into the consequences and accept responsibility for them. Then again, running into the will of a God full of love and grace is definitely not the worst thing that can happen! God has the power to redeem wrong decisions.

Bill and I have been married for nearly 23 years. We enjoy a unique relationship in marriage and ministry. Not only am I his wife but also co-pastor with him of our church. Our relationship resembles what I believe God desires for order in the church and home.

God has blessed us with unity. Seldom do Bill and I encounter situations over which we strongly disagree, but when we do I gladly allow Bill to try his way first. He has never once said to me in 23 years of marriage, "Melinda, submit to me on this." We just operate that way. He would never ask me, in the name of submission, to violate my conscience or disobey the Lord or Scripture. And I, in turn, am comfortable respecting him as the head of our home. Any issues that require yielding are insignificant things that fall into the category of methods of operating. Because he respects and honors me, Bill honors my opinion, believing God has sent me to help him.

Submission means operating within mutually agreed upon boundaries for marriage. There are areas of our marriage in which Bill wants me to initiate choices, such as what groceries to buy or where we go on vacation. I, in turn, could care less about what parts we need for the car or which bank we should use. We trust each other. In respecting him as the head, I consult him about anything I know he might want to decide, and he gives me the same right, allowing me to collaborate in decision-making.

I doubt that any Christian woman married to a man like Bill would have difficulty with submission!

The Christian wife's role is to submit to or harmonize with her husband. Accordingly, her husband's needs, strengths and weaknesses will define her role. To make rigid, blanket statements about a woman's role in her home does not allow for the individuality characteristic of each relationship. There is nothing biblical about all wives serving their husbands the same way. If a couple are happiest with the husband cooking and the wife working on the car (and we know such a couple), they should not feel as though they have stepped outside of divine order! Marriage should bring out the best in a man and woman, not squeeze them into constrictive molds.

Love is the ingredient that causes headship, submission and God's government to work anywhere. When it is absent, no amount of legalistic role definition will bring peace into the home.

A Woman's Place with the Children

About ten years ago, my sister and I spent the night with a family near a town in Ohio where I was speaking the next day. Lily, the woman of the house (whom we had not met), was not yet home, but her oldest son, Dan, greeted us at the door. We set our bags in the guest bedroom of the large frame farmhouse and returned to the kitchen, where Dan had put on the teapot. He apparently hoped a cup of tea would hold us until his mother came home!

We could tell by his appearance that Dan, in his early twenties, was following the beat of another drummer. He was dressed in a gauze shirt, faded blue jeans and sandals. With his dark brown hair pulled back into a ponytail, he truly looked like a holdover from the hippie days. We could tell from the things he wanted to talk about that he was not a Christian yet.

But one thing he said caught me by surprise: "You're really gonna love my mother." And in the next few minutes he talked about how he loved his parents, even though we could tell that philosophically they were miles apart.

The rest of the night we came to understand why. Lily and Harold loved their children unconditionally. Gone was the pressure I had felt in other homes I had visited where the children resented their parents' conversions. Some of these kids had been teenagers by the time their parents accepted the Lord, and they did not want to follow.

Dan was not ready, either, but apparently felt no parental pressure to conform; he felt loved the way he was—ponytail, motorcycle and all. God was free to do the saving.

The happy atmosphere in their home could not have been more genuine. We sat around the table eating home-cooked farm food, laughing and talking about "normal" things. It was one of the most enjoyable evenings of my life. Never have I felt more comfortable being just who I am.

As I lay awake that night in Lily's guest room, I tried to put my finger on what was different here. Lily and Harold did not seem embarrassed that Dan was not saved. They did not feel the need to explain his dress or behavior to us, as though their older son were the thermometer of their own spirituality. In fact, Dan's emotional condition, far more than his spiritual condition, reflected his parents' spiritual maturity. He was accepted by them without having to change. Nor was there conflict evident between Dan and his brother, Jake, a Christian and a delightful young man, for the affections of their parents.

It was obvious that neither of them had been compared negatively with the other.

I changed my message for the meeting the next day, using Dan's statement "You're really gonna love my mother." And God moved in the meeting, softening women's hearts and releasing them to love their children without having to change them. There was scarcely a dry eye in the room. Lily was a little embarrassed, but her friends at the meeting knew it was true. It was why they preferred her house as guest quarters for visiting speakers: There was a special presence of the Lord there.

Lily had overcome the sense of disgrace that many women experience when their children do not choose to follow the Lord. She did not seem to feel the sting of spiritual barrenness that afflicts many women whose children are not saved.

My sister and I cried the next day when we had to leave Lily and Harold's home. We felt as though we had been with our closest relatives. Even though everyone there was not a Christian, Jesus lived there.

A mother's often unconditional love is one of humanity's closest mirrors of God's love for each individual. Love does not demand performance; it just accepts. Love mends the damage done by the enemy. It restores the simplicity of the Gospel and the enjoyment of life to every relationship.

I have no doubt that Dan has long since come to Jesus, but what he decides will not affect Lily's walk with God. She has successfully detached her spirituality from his salvation and accepted the unconditional love of God as the fruit God wants her to bear. Lily is collaborating with the Lord to reveal the love of God in her marriage and with her children.

According to the Great Commission, Jesus is sending every believer out from the confines of home and enlarging his or her parameters of ministry, past the home to the uttermost parts of the earth. To say that every woman is called only to her home conflicts with the Lord's right to use any believer where He sees fit. Every believer is given spiritual gifts to be released as a manifestation of God's love to the Church.

The role of every Christian woman is individually suited to her and those to whom God is calling her to demonstrate His love. Her gifts from Him, both natural and spiritual, are clues to her kind of ministry. Every Christian woman, regardless of her marital status, has a ministry beyond the confines of her home, whether it is preaching the Gospel in a foreign country or witnessing to her friend next door.

A Woman's Place in the Church

When a woman's boundaries are too tightly defined, she feels trapped. When her freedoms and privileges are reduced and options erased, she feels crowded into a mold. Nowhere is this more evident than in the Church.

In Isaiah 54 God speaks a prophetic word to barren women today:

> "Shout for joy, O barren one, you who have borne no child; break forth into joyful shouting and cry aloud, you who have not travailed; for the sons of the desolate one will be more numerous than the sons of the married woman," says the Lord. "Enlarge the place of your tent; stretch out the curtains of your dwellings, spare not; lengthen your cords, and strengthen your pegs. For you will spread abroad to the right and to the left. And your descendants will possess nations, and they will resettle the desolate cities. Fear not, for you will not be put to shame. . . ."
>
> Isaiah 54:1–4

Have you noticed that when the birth of Jesus was imminent, there was a marked rise in the spiritual activity of women? For hundreds of years before Jesus' birth, no woman had prophesied. Yet after Jesus' birth Elizabeth, a barren woman, Mary, a virgin, and Anna, a widow, began to sing and prophesy. The time of the birth of the Messiah had arrived, the promised Savior who would crush the serpent's head. God would use the seed of woman and fulfill the promise He had made originally to Eve.

It was the traditions of God-fearing men that demeaned the position of women. Through deception and accusation, Satan twisted the Word of God with prejudice and rigidly imposed tradition to restrict her spiritual borders to no more than the confines of her house. According to the Talmud (the collection of ancient rabbinical writings in Judaism), woman was a piece of property. Suffering for the sin of Eve, she had to cover her head in disgrace and stand robbed of all God originally intended for her.

The Mishnah (the first section of the Talmud) demeaned woman further to nothing more than "a piece of meat . . . which one may eat, salt, roast partially or wholly cook." Participation in spiritual pursuits was forbidden. "It is a shame for a woman to let her voice be heard among men. . . . The voice of woman is filthy nakedness." A well-known rabbi added, "Let the words of the law be burned rather than committed to women."

These men who spent their lives studying the Law were deaf to all but tradition. They let tradition define women's borders to be far less than what God intended them to be.

Jesus faced these men so set in their ways. And though it threatened His ministry, He exposed their prejudice and hard-heartedness. "You nicely set aside the commandment of God," He told them, "in order to keep your tradition" (Mark 7:9).

Jesus' ministry marked a new day for women. Departing from rabbinical tradition and being full of grace and truth, He allowed women to sit at His feet and learn from Him. A company of women followed Him and paid his expenses out of their own means. Women were among His close friends, although not (for reasons, I believe, of sexual propriety) among the Twelve. Violating the custom of the day, Jesus initiated conversations with women—on one occasion, with a heathen Samaritan woman who came to a well where He was sitting. And on the day of His resurrection, He chose to appear first to Mary Magdalene, the only disciple who followed Him to the end, instructing her to go and impart the revelation of the resurrection.

Jesus knew exactly what He was doing. He was making a statement that contradicted the teaching of the rabbis. Jesus did more for women's rights in three years than any organized effort in all time! And He expects the Church to follow suit.

It has not been an easy struggle. But as women find their place in the Church today in both ministry and leadership, we find that an end-time harvest is ripening before us. God is healing the Church of her wounds and restoring her to health so that she will be spotless in the eyes of her Master on His return. Since part of His purpose includes using women to proclaim Christ as the victor over sin in every arena of life, God is enlarging the borders of her tent to include not only the marriage and home but also the Church. In all these places, He intends to remove a wounded woman's barrenness and restore her to a place of ministry where her natural and spiritual fruit can be borne without hindrance.

Finding Your Ministry

Your ministry is defined by the combination of natural talents and spiritual gifts God has placed within you. There are, according to the apostle Paul, varieties of gifts and ministries (1 Corinthians 12:4–5). If you are confused about what your ministry is, think what you were doing the last time you sensed the pleasure of God.

Your ministry will energize you and, though you may have times when the details drive you crazy, you will have the overall sense that God is pleased. This is how missionaries like Amy Carmichael can live in India for 55 years: The sense of God's pleasure is edifying. Your ministry will be developed by God in wilderness experiences, through hardship and suffering, through abundance and loss, through joy. But if you overcome the obstacles and learn to exercise your gifts, they will open the way for you. "A man's gift makes room for him, and brings him before great men" (Proverbs 18:16). It is not necessary to push your way in when God is raising you up; it will happen in His time.

When I had a deeper experience with the Lord some years ago, I got the distinct impression He wanted me to write. Having no idea how that should come about, I tucked the impression inside and prayed about it only rarely. In 1981 a minister prophesied out of the blue that I would write books for the Body of Christ.

Eight years later while teaching a women's retreat in Lincoln, Virginia, I met Sandy and Len LeSourd. Through their encouragement and friendship, the Lord opened a door at Chosen Books. Then I better understood the verse in Proverbs, "A man's gift makes room for him."

Similarly, although the Lord has opened doors for me to teach in many states, I have never initiated one contact for a speaking engagement. I just obeyed God where He put me alongside my husband in a small church in Pittsburgh, and He did the rest.

No woman need ever push her way into God's best for her, but overcoming the same spirit that afflicted Timothy in his ministry may move internal barriers that loom like giants, locking your ministry into a trap of timidity.

Timothy was young when he was set in charge of the church at Ephesus, particularly in comparison to the apostle

Paul, whose reputation preceded him everywhere. Following in Paul's footsteps was not easy, especially for a meek young man raised by a godly mother and grandmother. A father's influence in Timothy's life is not mentioned in the Bible. Perhaps that is why Paul took such an interest in him.

Pastoring in Ephesus brought out the best and worst in Paul's young protégé. False teachers, silly women, contentious people and those who mocked his youth rose up against him, intimidating him out of the place God had given him.

Paul knew what he needed: "Kindle afresh the gift of God which is in you through the laying on of my hands. For God has not given us a spirit of timidity, but of power and love and discipline [sensibility]" (2 Timothy 1:6–7). To drive out the giants of timidity that threatened him, Timothy needed to stir up the gift of the Holy Spirit he had received when Paul had ordained him.

The Holy Spirit within is equal to the task without when you are living in the boundaries of the inheritance God has given you. There is no need to push or become engaged in conflict. Just stir up the Holy Spirit within you, seek to edify the Church, and the power of God will make a path for you.

Now let's see what a woman must do to take the place God has assigned her.

Taking Your Place

Wandering in the wilderness while everyone was talking about the lands they would acquire on entering Canaan was beginning to trouble four women whose father had already died in the wilderness. Afraid that their escape from Egypt and wilderness struggle would result only in their poverty once Israel's invasion was successful, the five sisters—Tirzah, Hoglah, Mahlah, Noah and Milcah—found the courage to go to Moses himself about the matter.

Their spunk is recorded in Numbers 27. This may have been the first women's rights demonstration! They knew there was not much time left before Israel would take the land, and they wanted this matter settled before influential men in the tribe saw to it that they were left out of an inheritance altogether. Approaching Moses and Eleazar the priest, and boldly violating tradition, they carefully constructed the points of their argument and made their way to the place of judgment.

All these women wanted was a place among the other descendants of Joseph. Their father, Zelophehad, had died in the wilderness, but he had not been part of the rebellion of Korah, dying rather for his own sin.

"Why should the name of our father be withdrawn from among his family because he had no son?" the women implored. "Give us a possession among our father's brothers."

Their request must have made it past the elders, since it was highly unusual. Who had ever heard of women asking for rights to property? What an expression of faith! Their request was for property no one had seen, moreover, property some men doubted would ever be owned by Israelites.

Moses must have been puzzled, too, because he took their case before the Lord. And the Lord spoke to Moses directly about them: "The daughters of Zelophehad are right in their statements. You shall surely give them a hereditary possession among their father's brothers, and you shall transfer the inheritance of their father to them" (Numbers 27:7).

What if the women had never asked? What would have happened to them when the tribe of Manasseh took its place outside the gate of the land? Would they have been lost in the shuffle?

Look at another example, from the settling of the Promised Land, of a woman taking her God-assigned place.

When Israel invaded the land God had promised them, Caleb was the only Jew besides Joshua to have entered the land before. Caleb was a visionary who had doubtless been able to impart the vision for the land to his children. The land Caleb was given was no easy possession, but he swore to take the country the giants held. And to the man who captured one of the giants' cities that stood in his way, Caleb gave his daughter Achsah as a wife.

Before riding off with her husband, Achsah alighted from her donkey and asked her father for a field. Caleb gave her the Negev, a flat but dry territory.

Then Achsah, obviously possessed with the "different spirit" the Lord had seen in her father, persisted, "Give me a blessing; since you have given me the land of the Negev, give me also springs of water" (Joshua 15:19).

So Caleb gave Achsah the upper and lower springs.

Achsah's asking made all the difference between barrenness and fruitfulness. And asking made all the difference in the inheritance the five women received.

Rise up, woman! And take possession of the restoration and ministry God has for you.

Endnotes

Chapter 4

1. Popsy Sadock, "Domestic Abuse: Breaking the Violent Cycle" (Greensburg, Pa.: *The Tribune-Review*, April 15, 1992), Section E, pp. 1–2.

Chapter 7

1. Tim LaHaye, *Your Temperament: Discover Its Potential* (Wheaton, Ill.: Tyndale House Publishers, Inc., 1984), p. 18.
2. LaHaye, p. 17.
3. Bushnell, pp. 39, 41.

Bibliography

Briscoe, Stuart. "The Biblical Woman: We've Buried a Treasure." *Moody Monthly*, February 1983, p. 6.

Bushnell, Katherine C. *God's Word to Women*. North Collins, N.Y.: Ray B. Munson, privately published, no date, reprint of old book.

Cho, Paul Y. "Cho Speaks Out on Women in Ministry." *Ministries Today*, November-December 1991, p. 102.

LaHaye, Tim. *Your Temperament: Discover Its Potential*. Wheaton, Ill.: Tyndale House Publishers, Inc., 1984.

Martin, William A. *Prophet with Honor: The Billy Graham Story*. New York: William Morrow & Co., Inc., 1991.

McPeak, Dave. *Post-Traumatic Stress Syndrome*. Pittsburgh: Vet Center, February 1981.

Penn-Lewis, Jessie. *The Magna Charta of Woman*. Minneapolis: Bethany Fellowship, 1975.

Penn-Lewis, Jessie. *War on the Saints*. New York: Thomas E. Lowe, Ltd., 1979.

Price, Dr. Charles S. *The Real Faith*. Springdale, Pa.: Whitaker House (distributors), 1968.

Sadock, Popsy. "Domestic Abuse: Breaking the Violent Cycle." Greensburg, Pa.: *The Tribune-Review*, April 5, 1992, Section E, pp. 1–2.

Stanley, Dr. Charles. *Eternal Security: Can You Be Sure?* Nashville: Oliver Nelson, 1990.

Trombley, Charles. *Who Said Women Can't Teach?* South Plainfield, N.J.: Bridge Publishing, 1985.

Tucker, Ruth A. *From Jerusalem to Irian Jaya: A Biographical History of Christian Missions.* Grand Rapids: Academie Books, Zondervan Publishing House, 1983.